get your mind on...
YOUR PEOPLE

get your mind on...
YOUR PEOPLE

Becoming
the Organization
Everyone Wants
to Work For

LORI STOHS
Human Capital Strategist

First published by Transcendent Publishing

Copyright © 2017 by Lori Stohs

First Edition

Transcendent Publishing

PO Box 66202

St. Pete Beach, FL 33736

PH: (800) 232-5087

www.transcendentpublishing.com

www.loristohs.com/getyourmindon

Cover Design: StyleMatters, LLC, info@style-matters.com

Interior Design: StyleMatters, www.style-matters.com

ISBN-10: 0-9993125-4-5

ISBN-13: 978-0-9993125-4-4

Printed in the United States of America on acid-free paper

14 15 16 17 18 19   10 9 8 7 6 5 4 3 2 1

I dedicate this book to the leaders who believed in me, the mentors who gave their valuable time and honest feedback to me, and the clients who trusted me—and most important to Ethan and Emily, who gave me the motivation to follow my mission and purpose.

TABLE OF CONTENTS

INTRODUCTION

What's the pulse of your organization? The inside. The soul. Do you really know underneath all the hustle and bustle of day-to-day business about your biggest investment? About the most valuable investment you'll ever make...your people...your human capital?

Perhaps more important: Do you know how people are really feeling? Are your employees engaged, committed, and loyal? Are they engaging your customers with every interaction? Are you aware of what's happening in your organization at the soul level? Is the pulse healthy, consistent, and steady or racing with anxiety and dying?

Charles, a CEO of a large, international organization, felt he had a handle on his business. While there were highs and lows with the normal business cycles, he felt confident that he had his finger on the pulse, on the soul of the organization. Business results were on the rise except for a few blips in a few business units due to the economy. Charles felt things were going well until he started asking questions, really listening to his people, and pulling the layers back. What he discovered was that as the organization had grown, management had remained lean so some of his managers were not getting enough time with their people.

At his biannual, three-day offsite leadership conference with his top leaders, Charles always challenged them to think differently about the business. He did that again this year but he added some special guests. So one afternoon these special guests of all ages and roles dressed in their business-casual work attire and began to speak. Each had a story—a personal story that captured the leaders' attention, not because they were stellar stories about their engagement but about how poorly they were mistreated in the organization. Sad as it may be, these were current and previous employees of the company. The leaders were in shock; they were numb and some even tearful. No one knew this was happening. Not in their organization. Deep underneath the hustle and bustle of it all, part of their soul was dying.

Think not only about what these people experienced circumstantially in their roles at this company, but about the psychological damage they might have experienced—the potential insecurity and lack of confidence. The fear, the anxiety, the stress. Think about how this might have affected their health, their children, and their families. When we do not truly value our people within the organization, we don't just affect the bottom line, we affect homes and communities.

This is a book about raising leaders' consciousness about their human capital and the realization that this capital—their people—is the most valuable asset their organization could possibly have. It helps leaders see how critical it is that we engage our people by putting them in roles that match their talents, give them a great manager, help them grow as individuals, and align the work to support our organizational strategies. Engaged employees aligned with the right business strategy lead to world-class performance. When you get your mind on your people, seemingly intractable issues can resolve. And when things go well at work, that helps at home too. Human capital consciousness makes for better organizations, and a better world. It is a healthy place to be.

Now, many of you already know that your people are valuable. You may even be feeling you are taking some actions to help your people excel, and yet you may be wondering why you are not seeing consistent results across your organization. This book will provide you awareness of what actions you can engage in to shift your organization to new levels and to achieve consistent

> **Shift your organization to new levels by getting your mind on your human capital.**

performance by getting your mind on your human capital; I call it developing your human capital consciousness. It will provide you with a clear guide on how to transform your workforce across the board, so that high performance is not an anomaly or a mystery, but a known entity that you see consistently throughout the organization from top to bottom.

Using the philosophy and tools in this book, you will have the capacity to create a culture of consciousness and the right organizational structure to align with your people and your business strategy. You will be able to choose the right people for the right roles and engage them. You will be able to build high-functioning teams where individuals can shine and the team can produce results. You will be able to remove obstacles that allow new efficiencies to be realized and employee creativity and innovation to flow.

By the time you are done reading this book, you will have more than a new tool in your tool kit or a new weapon in your arsenal. Whether you are a conceptual leader, an executive who leads from the heart, one who relies on the analytics, or a person who leads by doing, you will have a whole new awareness about the value of your people and how to use this awareness to lead, manage, and leverage your people to sky-scrape through company goals and raise your organization to new heights. You will have, too, a practical and comprehensive model—the Human Capital Optimization Model—to operationally engage your people in their work and the organization's mission from start to finish (and start again!), allowing you to make sure your people are awake and executing at their highest capacity and your organization is reaching its goals. By getting your mind on your people, you can achieve the results you desire and leave a legacy.

Ready to get started?

IS THE MODEL RIGHT FOR YOU?

Could the Human Capital Optimization Model help your organization? Do you have challenges that indicate your organization could benefit from its implementation? Conducting an employee engagement assessment or culture assessment can provide clarity on your current organizational state and indicate whether the model could be useful. For now, as a shortcut, if you can answer yes to any of the following questions, the Human Capital Optimization Model might be right for your organization:

- Would you like to increase employee productivity?
- Would you like to increase the consistency of the delivery of your product or service?
- Would you like to reduce employee turnover and/or absenteeism?
- Would you like to improve the effectiveness of your managers?
- Would you like to know how to select good managers?
- Would you like to increase customer engagement?
- Would you like to reduce workplace conflict?
- Would you like to increase employee engagement?
- Would you like to do a better job hiring and promoting the right people?

If you answered yes to any of the previous questions and want to become serious about solving these problems, I would encourage you to read further and see how the Human Capital Optimization Model can help you. Start by evaluating your organization and determining whether your people strategy and business strategy are in alignment (see chapter 2).

If you have not measured your employee engagement, doing so would help you get a sense of what key issues are looming within the organization and could give you a good target to start with instead of guessing. Too many organizations know they have a problem but are not sure how to fix it or where to start, or they really don't understand its root cause. When they spend a lot of money in an attempt to fix the perceived issue, that "fix" usually ends up being a Band-Aid that comes off quickly and does not represent a sustainable solution. By taking a holistic approach and being aware of the people who underpin and execute the strategy, you will be able to get to the heart of the issue and make sustainable change.

Don't we all have the desire to be engaged and awake? At an individual employee level, doesn't everyone want to have a job they love and do well at? At a leadership level, doesn't every executive, manager, and director want employees to come to work happy and ready to work? Today you may have heard this attitude described as *employee engagement*, a phenomenon that has been shown to link clearly with positive business results. Now, I am going to push us to go even further than engagement, to seeking a state of being alive and awake. I am on a mission to awaken your *human capital consciousness*: a keen awareness of the humanity within our employees and their powerful value to the organization and, in turn, to a greater place, its impact on our community and the world.

Many of you know the value of your people and simply need the tools to operationalize this understanding and take it to another level. The Human Capital Optimization Model will provide these to you. From branding to hiring to mentoring, it will walk you through the key elements you need when launching a new department or fixing a broken division. In short, this model will help to ensure that your business strategy is supported by a well-thought-out people strategy. It will help you create and foster an organization of employees that perform at their best and enjoy the journey. How amazing is that?!

I am passionate about getting people engaged, awake, and able to perform at their best. I am passionate about helping leaders and managers make decisions and create structures that allow each individual performer to shine. Why? Every day, while consulting in organizations and as a consumer receiving goods and services, I see such a disparity among the individual employees who make up organizations. I see a small percentage of people who are fully engaged and

> **I am on a mission to awaken your *human capital consciousness*: a keen awareness of the humanity within our employees and their powerful value to the organization.**

consistent in their performance, and I see many other people sleepwalking through their day. This isn't right. This lack of engagement is affecting not just our organizations but our society. We don't need to settle for so little when the solution is right in front of us.

When I have the privilege to see an organization that is performing at a high level, I study it and seek to understand what's different about it. When I meet certain employees who are highly engaged and performing, I pay attention to what's working well as compared with their disengaged counterparts. Overall, I reflect on how we can get more organizations to be at this world-class level. In this book, I bring to bear my eighteen years of experience and knowledge as a Principal, Founder, Chief People Officer, and Human Capital Consultant in many industries, so that you no longer have to scratch your head and wonder why only some employees are superstars. With the knowledge and discoveries provided in this book, you can consciously cultivate an engaged and awake organization. I hope you will join me in thinking about your organization and how we can all do this together.

So, get ready to become awake. It is time to get your mind on your human capital in a new way, with a deeper level of consciousness. It is time to go beyond the mentality of dry, corporate work locked up in an office building that is somehow separate from our humanness. It is time to remember that, yes, even at work, we ourselves are alive *on this planet,* as are our employees.

We are not just automatons going through the motions—or at least we don't deserve to be—we are talented, creative beings, each with our own unique contributions to make to the benefit of the whole. It is a privilege to have each and every day to do good work together, for ourselves, our families, our communities, our country, and our world. This book is going to challenge you to become awake to your own energy as a leader and to the incredible capacity you have to awaken your people to do their very best work.

Figure 0.1–Human Capital Concepts Defined

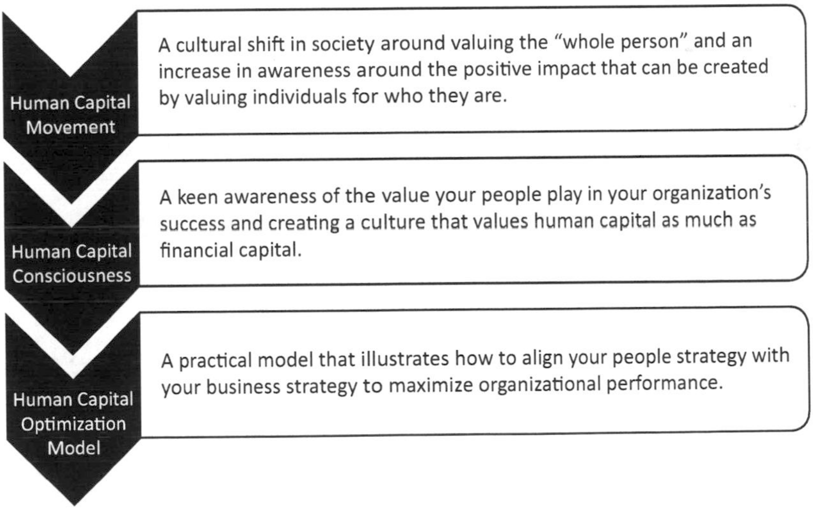

Human Capital Movement
A cultural shift in society around valuing the "whole person" and an increase in awareness around the positive impact that can be created by valuing individuals for who they are.

Human Capital Consciousness
A keen awareness of the value your people play in your organization's success and creating a culture that values human capital as much as financial capital.

Human Capital Optimization Model
A practical model that illustrates how to align your people strategy with your business strategy to maximize organizational performance.

HOW TO USE THIS BOOK

As you read through this book, I invite you to use it in the way that works best for you. You will discover that it contains conceptual ideas for leaders and high-level thinkers as well as nuts-and-bolts practical guidance for those in the workplace who are in charge of executing the work. If you need one aspect of this book but not the other, feel free to skip those sections that don't apply to you, or enjoy reading from start to finish to get the full benefit of the book. There is plenty to discover, from the human capital optimization philosophy, research statistics, and workplace anecdotes, to "Get Your Hands On" exercises and "More to Get Your Mind On" bonus material on the web (www.loristohs.com/getyourmindon).

PART I

get your mind on...

YOUR
HUMAN
CAPITAL

Engaged employees go home and positively influence their friends, families, and communities, and that's good for all of us.

WHERE ARE WE HEADING?

The Human Capital Movement

Bit by bit, the organizational world is waking up to the importance of every individual. We see it in the trend toward employee-friendly policies in the workplace. I think about the haircuts and dry cleaning services available on Google's campus, 3M's 15 percent time (during which employees are allowed to devote on-the-clock time to ideas they have for new products—thank 15 percent time for Post-It Notes!), and Epic's paid month-long sabbatical that employees are eligible for every five years.[1] In the business media, we hear about the importance of keeping our employees engaged and of valuing their talent and strengths. More and more, people are being treated like they matter at work.

How has your workplace handled the pull to transform into a more humane employer? Have you answered the call, shied away, or run away like your hair was on fire? Whether you have been on the cutting edge in leading the way with employee-friendly improvements or you have held stubbornly to more traditional HR policies, feeling reluctant to coddle your people, I am going to offer you a more nuanced understanding of how to design your workplace to be human friendly. We are going to go beyond perks and flexible scheduling, because those items are mere consolation prizes to employees who are not positively engaged in their work. I will help you get your mind on a human-centered approach that is one that we can all stand behind, because it serves both the person *and* the organization. In the end, it serves the community in a greater way, too, because happy and engaged employees go home and positively influence their friends, families, and communities, and that's good for all of us.

WAKE UP YOUR HUMAN CAPITAL CONSCIOUSNESS AND GET YOUR PEOPLE ENGAGED

People-friendly policies like casual Fridays and luxurious employee cafeterias can be nice and are very attractive in competitive environments for recruiting talent—very few employees will complain about being given more freedom or perks—but I am going to challenge you to take your approach to valuing and leveraging your people to a deeper level. I'm talking instead about digging into the bones of your organization and making sure it is structured in a way that engages your employees in work they are great at so they can perform at their peak and you can see business results every day, both in the employees' output and on the bottom line.

The state of employee engagement today is disappointing (see Figure 1.1). Gallup indicates that typically in the United States

- 32 percent of people are *fully engaged* in their work every day
- 51 percent of people are *disengaged* in their work
- 17 percent of people are *actively disengaged*[2]

When the *fully engaged* individuals come to work, they love their jobs. Their jobs are their lives. They're building, they're creating, they are consistently performing well, and they're very interested in the work that they do. Even if that employee is somebody in the mail room, if that employee is fully engaged, he or she loves what he or she is doing—every day. These employees have passion and they're productive. And because they are engaged, they're very engaging to those around them as well. The snowballs you want your company to produce get made and they roll downhill, getting bigger as they go, reaching their full potential. It's a win–win for employees and employers.

> **When the fully engaged individuals come to work, they love their jobs.**

As for the disengaged folks (the

51 percent), those are the ones for whom some days are good and some days are bad. They come in and make the doughnuts, day after day, put in their eight hours, and take a long lunch once in a while. They have some great times when they are really energized and some not-so-great times when they are drained. It's inconsistent, and inconsistency is never good for the organization. It's a sometimes-win, sometimes-lose situation for employees and employers, three steps forward and two steps back or, even worse, the reverse: two steps forward, three steps back. In this light, you can see how disengagement can hack away at productivity and profits.

As for those who are actively disengaged (the 17 percent), these individuals are breaking down the walls of anything good we're trying to do in any organization. The engaged employees are building the walls up; the disengaged are tearing them down. It's not pretty and is most definitely a lose–lose situation all around.

I quit taking my clothes to a certain local dry cleaner because I was there literally every week and the woman at the counter treated me like a stranger. Each time I walked in, she looked at me like she'd never seen me before. It was almost bizarre. I was interacting with this same woman every seven days or so. Every visit, I smiled and tried to make small talk with her. The likely explanation for the glazed look on her face each time I walked in was disengagement. She was aloof to all the customers, not just me. Conclusion? It was not the right job for her. Even kids understand the concept of engagement and disengagement.

When mine were younger, they would say, "Mom, that person's not in the right job, he's not very happy" or "Gosh, he really loves his job."

Figure 1.1: Employee Engagement in the Workplace

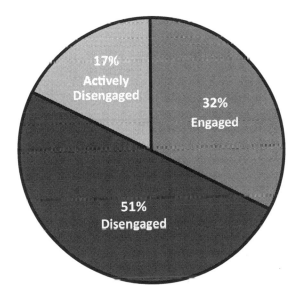

Most organizations' workforces reflect the degree of engagement shown in Figure 1.1 in some way, shape, or form. No matter where you are in your organization, there is likely to be lots of disengagement. That's why when you go to a store, even a big-box or chain store where you'd expect a certain consistency in the experience, you will get inconsistent customer service depending on the day, the visit, or the department as a result of this consistently low engagement at work. Very rarely will I find over 50 percent of an organization fully engaged. That means in the best cases, I will find that only one out of two employees is fully engaged—only half of the organization! And that's best case. More typically, it's only one out of three employees, or one-third of an organization, that's fully engaged. And what a shame this is! People spend most of their waking hours on the job in some way. Why wouldn't we, as employers, want to understand how to engage employees? It's not only a matter of what we can get from our employees—and don't get me wrong, engagement brings with it tremendous productivity benefits—but it's something we can give to the people without whom our organization would not function. Your people are your greatest asset, so treat them like the treasures they are!

The Human Capital Optimization model gives you straightforward ways to engage your employees. It works like this. You start by making sure your people are in roles that align with their talents, natural behaviors, and experience. That gives you a great foundation for engagement. Without this foundation, things like nice pay increases, useful feedback from one's manager, or a cool, fun environment will not be enough to make an employee feel fulfilled. Ultimately, what I am challenging you to do is to heighten your organization's *human capital consciousness*: its ability to be aware at all times of the impact the decisions you make have on the people who play a role in the success and challenges of your organization.

When you are in tune to your human capital consciousness, you are going to know what you and your people need to do on a regular basis to perform their jobs at peak performance levels that support desired business outcomes—preventing unnecessary problems before they happen, helping the organization to run at its smoothest, and providing consistent results that please customers, management, the board, and shareholders alike.

A lot of leaders, managers, and HR professionals are already doing great things in organizations for their people. Although benefits and perks can be helpful in recruiting new employees, in my view, without the depth of valuing your people, they are mostly window dressing when it comes to keeping employees engaged and the organization running well. Once on the job, if someone is doing work that they aren't good at or they have a manager beating them down every day, no amount of goodies can overcome those challenges to keep employees engaged.

> **Although benefits and perks can be helpful in recruiting new employees, without the depth of valuing your people, they are mostly window dressing when it comes to keeping employees engaged.**

What I say is this: Keep the perks, but go deeper. Focus on the whole person and the whole job, and how these two fit well together. This will bring about the change you are desiring. And if you are already feeling good about your organization today and aiming to move to great, getting your mind on your people and their roles in this way will help you fine tune to get there. It's time to wake up your human capital consciousness! (For an introduction to the Human Capital Movement, visit www.loristohs.com)

TRUE ENGAGEMENT LEADS TO CONSISTENT PERFORMANCE

When individuals are fully engaged at work (the 32 percent), they're consistent. They're consistently meeting their responsibilities, consistently creating new ways of doing things, consistently filling their roles, and consistently performing at a high level. The team and the company can count on them.

Because individuals in the disengaged group (the 51 percent) have some good days and some bad days, they are not consistent. They are motivated to work on some projects but not others; they perform at high levels sometimes but not others. It's spotty, and the organization doesn't get all it needs out of these individuals to be successful.

As for the actively disengaged individuals—those people who are miserable, counterproductive, and dismantling everything that everyone else is trying to build—they are consistent but on the bad side: they consistently assume the worst and perform poorly, and they try to bring others down with them. Trapped in the past, uncomfortable with change, these folks think the world is against them and nobody likes them; we create a new idea, and they're the cancer spreading rumors through the department to eat away at these new ideas so they flop. Think of the word *drama*.

Employee productivity, product quality, and customer service are logical initial victims of poor engagement in the workplace—if someone doesn't want to be on the job, what are the odds of their doing the job right, or even doing the job? Although the workday might be eight, nine, or ten hours long, truth be told, disengaged workers are only productive for a fraction of that time. According to a recent Gallup report,[3] engaged employees spend an average of 4.5 hours of a workday in *flow*—Mihaly Czikszentmihalyi's description of a state in which an activity is so engaging and all-encompassing that time flies by;[4] disengaged employees average 2.7 hours in such a state. And that assumes disengaged workers get to the workplace at all: absenteeism and illness (often attributable to stress and unhappiness brought on by a detested job) keep disengaged workers at home a greater percentage of the time compared with their more engaged peers. Disengaged workers' absence may be for the good in some cases, as safety incidents are almost 70 percent more common among disengaged than engaged workers.[5]

Think about that for a moment. A bad role or team fit at work doesn't have just an emotional effect: it can have a completely unintended outcome with serious, real-world consequences. In other words, not only can disengaged workers sabotage your organization's product or service output, but they may also be putting themselves and others in physical danger. As you get your mind on your people—making sure they are in the right roles and that these roles align with your business goals—engagement and consistent performance can follow.

SAVING DOLLARS THROUGH HUMAN CAPITAL OPTIMIZATION

One of the great things about the Human Capital Optimization approach is that it does not inherently cost your organization more money. In fact, chances are, it will even save you some. Some leaders with wonderful intentions identify problems without fully understanding the human side of things and then waste money trying to fix the wrong issues. By using the Human Capital Optimization Model provided in this book, you will have the structure you need to ensure that you examine the relevant people issues from the start, make the right fixes, and avoid costly mistakes or troubleshooting. I know of more than one leader who learned this process the hard way.

When Stephanie, a driven, energetic, and newly appointed CEO, joined a manufacturing company where sales were flat, she rolled up her sleeves and prepared to make changes to a culture that had become dull and complacent. Evaluating strategies, systems, and financials were a few of the major overhauls in the business cycle that needed to be completed. An additional, key focus was to reinvigorate sales numbers by addressing concerns regarding manufacturing times and product turnaround speed. At this point, millions of dollars had been spent on new initiatives and months had gone by. Yet the original issue had not improved. What would it take to connect with more customers and improve product sales?

By the time Stephanie called me, she said she had worked through many business solutions. She was grasping for any advice I could provide. I started by looking at the situation using my method of consulting that involves applying my human capital lens. I went straight to the source and asked more questions about the "who." *Who* was running the sales division? And was the *role defined* properly to meet the needs of the organization? Experience has taught me that many times issues that manifest at the ground level start at the top with the wrong person in a poorly defined role.

Using the Human Capital Optimization Model, we quickly discovered that the executive of the sales division needed to have a mind for developing strategy to meet the demands of a changing marketplace. Yet, this was an impossible thing to ask of him. Like all strengths and talents, strategic thinking is not something that can be taught. You either have it or you don't, and the executive of the sales division lacked this kind of thinking. He was great at building relationships and he knew the business. He was a good maintainer of what was built, but when the market changed and their sales were below projections quarter after quarter, he could not come up with the solution to shift the sales force to a new level. As a matter of fact, he was manipulating people due to his insecurities around his incapacity to meet the demands placed upon him.

After clearly redefining what job responsibilities the executive of the sales division needed in the current marketplace and seeing more clearly than ever that there was a mismatch between the needs of the job and the existing leader, we had to let him go and search for a replacement. While he had been a fit for what the organization needed years back, as the organization shifted, the role had outgrown him. A few months later, the new executive, who was clearly a fit for the defined role, was able to come in and take the organization to a new level by restructuring the sales organization. While the sales force is noticing a lot of change, they are all experiencing a new level of energy and engagement with the new executive, and the company is back on track to meet the sales goals. By getting our minds on the people—in this case the sales division executive—we were able to move through a seemingly intractable organizational challenge.

In working with organizations of all types—local, national, and international; small, medium, and large—and across a range of fields and industries and in being an executive of a 350-person startup, I have lived, seen, and heard the most common challenges that organizations face: lack of productivity, high turnover, conflict, poor managers, low customer engagement, low employee engagement, and finding the right people. Regardless of the organizational challenge or the type of organization, the source of most problems is ultimately the same: people. People are the root of the organization. They make the decisions. They create the processes, systems, and products.

With your human capital consciousness in tune, I want you to start to look at organizational concerns holistically. If you have detected problems with your product, consider how these problems may be a symptom of a larger problem involving the people leading and executing product manufacturing or development. If it's clear that your product is great through positive feedback from focus groups and you've pinpointed sales issues instead, examine the sales and marketing people strategy and structure.

> **What looks like an issue with the strategy or revenue may start with a people issue.**

When leadership hits a snag or a roadblock on the way to a

company goal, they often say things like, "This is a revenue issue," "We need to develop a new product," or "We need to cut expenses." At the end of the day, however, many leaders forget to look for the root cause of many of these issues, much less the biggest one that is right in front of them. Have you really looked at issues around the people who make your organization go? What looks like an issue with the strategy or revenue may start with a people issue.

This is not about scapegoating or blaming; there's often no true fault to be assigned: business needs continually change. Someone who was hired years ago for a particular role might find herself floundering in an unfamiliar role, which morphed over time into an unrecognizable new position when she wasn't paying attention. And if job roles change, you can bet that businesses have evolved over time too, and many a leader has not made adjustments to the business model to accommodate the changes.

Many leaders would be well-served by taking a long, self-reflecting look at whether their organization's current structure and alignment of strategies, departments, and goals are still optimized to achieve the group's stated goals. Sometimes we need to reevaluate our business model and strategies. Working under an outdated or misaligned system is not intentional, but doing so doesn't set our people or organization up for success.

A DEEPER DIVE INTO SOCIAL RESPONSIBILITY

Let's talk for a moment about what an organization should provide for its employees. A paycheck comes to mind, as does a safe work environment, but those are pretty much givens, basic expectations for the employer–employee relationship. The next level might be benefits. Here's a place, in fact, where you can get creative (on-site massage therapy, anyone?).

What if we took a step back, though, and looked at a passage by German educator Friedrich Fröbel, quoted in Eric Butterworth's book *Spiritual Economics:* "The delusive idea that men merely . . . work for the sake of preserving their bodies and procuring for themselves bread, houses, and clothes—is degrading, and not to be encouraged. The true origin of man's activity and creativeness lies in his increasing impulse to embody outside of himself the divine and spiritual element within him."[6]

Sit with that for a moment. Think of how much time your people spend on the job, how much of their day and their energy they pour into your company. Why *wouldn't* they want and need to find the deeper meaning in what they do for you? Says Eric Butterworth, "Work is, and should be so considered by every worker, a giving process."[7] How much more engaged will your employees be if your work gives them the opportunity to tap into their gifts, growing and sharing their skills and capabilities, making them feel like they're giving of themselves in such a way that they are able to not only self-actualize but also be a part of a worthy cause larger than themselves?

This kind of building up of your employees has an effect that extends far beyond the workplace. When employees feel like they are contributing, growing, and sharing something good, they are energized. They know they themselves have talents, skills, and experiences that can add value to their community outside of work, not just while they are on their employer's clock. Instead of coming home and collapsing or indulging in habits such as drinking, smoking, or overeating to numb or "reward" themselves after slogging through yet another dreary day at the office (or, worse, taking out their bad mood left over from a day of drudgery on their families), your people would have the confidence, energy, and desire to give of themselves to their friends, neighbors, clubs, churches, activities, and the like outside of work, acting as shining lights and contributors to the world. Are you still feeling confident that having free sodas in the break room is a top-notch perk, when you could go the extra mile and help foster thriving communities by creating happy, engaged human beings who are all here fulfilling their purpose? Are you serving your purpose as a leader? It starts at the top.

Consider, too, that employees who are engaged attract strong applicants to your company. When a job role opens up, you're going to have the best talent lining up to be considered for the position, because they're going to want to be part of your supportive, character-building workplace that is becoming the organization everyone wants to work for.

Empower your employees to contribute to their communities. Make your workplace great by providing more than salaries, benefits, and supportive managers: Go the extra mile to value them as a person. Says Butterworth, "Work should be an experience of growth."[8] That growth will benefit not just you, not just your employees, but the world. And isn't that a powerful legacy to leave?

CONCLUSION: CREATING A BETTER WORLD

It's tempting to try to turn organizational challenges into something other than a human capital issue, because people can be difficult. People can be hard to understand; they can be hard to get. People aren't machines: we are unique, we are alive, we are complex, and sometimes we are messy! It might be easier if we could just get rid of them, no? Don't tell me the thought hasn't crossed your mind once or twice. Is there a robotic solution? Fortunately, the moment you come to grips with the reality that it's all about the people is the moment you can be in tune with them and start doing things differently and better.

While each individual person is one of a kind, you can still put consistent, clear practices into place at work to get the best from your employees, making for a highly productive organization with an environment where employees are motivated, reliable, and productive. What's more, these practices will help you engage your people. Many people just want to be understood, and when they receive this understanding, oh, what a gift it is to them. When your people are engaged, it makes it more pleasurable to manage and mentor them, creating a reinforcing cycle of positivity and growth.

> **Many people just want to be understood, and when they receive this understanding, oh, what a gift it is to them.**

As the book unfolds, I walk you through these practices, providing explanations, guidance, and examples to help you and your organization get your mind on your people and follow the road to success. Chapters 2 and 3 provide the models I use every day with clients—the Human Capital Optimization Model and the Whole Person Model—to ensure that you are able to put people in the right roles and make sure these roles align with the business strategy. Soon enough, you can begin using these models at your organization, too, and reaping the benefits. Yes, people put processes into place, and I am going to help assure that they can do it well at your organization by providing everything you need to put the right people processes into action. No guessing needed.

What excites me most about working with companies to get their employees fully engaged and their people fully optimized is the ripple effects this can have on our world. Happier, productive workplaces lead to happier and healthy homes and communities, as engaged employees take the passion, focus, creativity, and joy that they feel at work into their family life and their communities. Engaged employees are fulfilled human beings who are not focused on numbing out by overeating, overdrinking, overspending, gossiping, gambling, or consuming too much reality TV and celebrity gossip magazines.

If you've ever seen a fulfilled and engaged employee at the end of the workday, you know that this employee looks a lot different from the employee who is unfulfilled at work and disengaged. Even when tired, the engaged one usually has a light in his eyes or a smile on his face, while the disengaged one probably has a sour expression on her face or a frantic energy that could set a room of people on edge. When these folks leave the office, that aura of positivity or negativity travels with them, affecting the world around them. In the book *Psychological Capital and Beyond*, the authors note that being preoccupied by negative thoughts and emotions—say, about the unengaging job one just left for the day—uses up one's capacity to experience other thoughts of any kind, positive or negative. In other words, the cloud of negativity a disengaged employee is carrying around "consumes the individual in negativity, taking attention away from those things that are positive."[9] That bad day at work ends up being followed by a bad night at home, because work has robbed the employee of the ability to see the good things around him.

Imagine instead a workplace that, through engagement, creates positive psychological capital that strengthens employees' soul base. Those employees are going to feel good and keep seeing the good around them even when they're off the clock, because work left them with the mental and emotional energy to appreciate the positive in all areas of their lives. Now, which employees would you prefer to cultivate?

In his book *Employee Engagement for Everyone*, employee engagement expert Kevin Kruse tells the story of what he calls "the best leadership compliment I ever got."[10] At a company social gathering, the wife of one of his employees came up to him and thanked him for improving her marriage. She said, "My husband used to come home and be so grumpy I wouldn't want to be around him. But since he started working for you, he went back to being the man I married."[II] Think about yourself and of some time that you were possibly in the same shoes as that husband. You didn't realize how bad it was at work until after you left that employer. The dysfunctional workplace changed you. When you think about it, such an effect makes perfect sense, but does anyone in company leadership think about how employees' lives outside of work will improve or suffer when making workplace policies? Maybe such considerations should be a regular part of the conversation!

To me, creating a workplace of engaged employees leads to the ultimate win–win. Engaged employees help organizations reach profitability, a fulfilled mission, and their fullest potential for success, and then these engaged employees leave the building and have a positive impact on our world. It's a powerful process that starts small and touches many lives along the way: mothers, fathers, sons, daughters, husbands, wives, friends, neighbors, and people in need. The truth is that we can get great profitability *and* a great society. In my view, this is not just a dream, but the wave of the future. This is the Human Capital Movement.

Build profitable organizations and increase the level of humanity in the workplace.

THE HUMAN CAPITAL OPTIMIZATION MODEL

Aligning Your People Strategy with Your Business Strategy

When the right people are in the right jobs, everyone wins. Employees feel engaged, customers feel taken care of, and leaders can rest easy knowing that their people are performing at their very best. No one wants to hate their job (well, maybe a few do). And customers don't want to work with people who don't like their work or are gasping for air, trying to keep their heads above water because they are out of their element. Why does the veil of work have to transform so many of us into cynics and deadbeats? I have been driven to champion the human capital movement because of the reality that far too many people are disengaged at work and that this is not good for our society and our world. I believe we can build profitable organizations *and* increase the level of humanity in the workplace.

The numbers do seem to tell us something about the state of things in the workplace today. In spite of the trend toward employee-friendly policies highlighted in the previous chapter, we know that two-thirds of the U.S. workforce is still disengaged.[1] What's more, only four in ten employees strongly agree that they get the opportunity to do what they do best on the job every day.[2] That's kind of scary. This means their strengths are being wasted and that they are likely not performing at the peak level desired by the organization. Many people who are hired are nice, show up to work, and seem responsible, but do they have the right talent for the role and are the expectations of their role clear? Many times, this is not the case, so our investment from the beginning is not a good one. We are getting inconsistent performance from them and likely extra drama that is costing the company a lot of money.

Another important reality to consider is this: over 50 percent of the managers leading those people shouldn't be in management roles.[3] If your organization is like most, more than half of the managers in charge have no business being in these roles because they do not have the talent needed to manage people. They have been promoted to management not because they have demonstrated great management skills such as communicating vision, delegating work, and developing people but because they are experts in their field—IT, sales, finance, and so on. Being a genius programmer, a top salesperson, or a financial wizard is different from being an excellent manager of people, but companies often promote on the basis of superstar expertise rather than the right talent to manage. In the end, we have too many managers who aren't good at managing in charge of people who aren't fully engaged in their work and who are not doing work that taps into their potential. It's a situation that's far less than ideal. And this too leads to inconsistent productivity! So are you nodding your head, saying, "Yes, I know we have this problem, but how can we fix it?" The how is in the Human Capital Optimization Model.

Why would any of us settle for anything less than people doing what they are good at? Don't we theoretically want the best surgeon performing our loved one's surgery, the best teacher teaching our children, and the law enforcement officer who is good at his job defending our children and our streets? It just makes sense to do what

> **The Human Capital Optimization Model is built around marrying your people strategy with your business strategy to create high performance that keeps people engaged and produces the world-class business results you desire.**

we can to make sure the person in the job is someone who is great at it. I designed the Human Capital Optimization Model to make sure we can do just that and have seen its positive effects.

Just imagine the rise in performance we would see within organizations if we leveraged our consciousness around our human capital and made sure that even 75 percent or 80 percent of managers were good at managing and that we had 80 percent or 85 percent of individuals working in the roles that tapped their strengths—where they could really perform and produce because they were doing what they were great at. Even at a level of 75 percent, we'd be looking at a really positive performance difference.

When you have the right people in the right roles, from marketing to operations, and they are being managed by individuals who know how to manage, you ensure that you will be able to get the very most out of your greatest assets—your people. These same people will remain engaged, giving to the organization with dedication and staying longer than they would if they were disengaged or miserable. Align your high-performing employees and managers to a solid business strategy, and you have just set your organization up for the ultimate success: increased customer engagement, a fulfilled mission, and ultimately profitability. The Human Capital Optimization Model is built around helping you do these very things: marrying your people strategy with your business strategy to create high performance that keeps people engaged and produces the world-class business results you desire.

A CLOSER LOOK AT THE MODEL

The Human Capital Optimization Model is a robust framework that I've developed on the basis of what I've learned from my work with Gallup, Microsoft, and many FORTUNE 500 companies over the past eighteen years to help organizations get the highest performance out of their people. Growing up in the business side of organizations, I quickly recognized there was often a gap between the business strategy and the people strategy of organizations. As I studied human behavior and organizational behavior, I noticed that the "people stuff" seemed to get set off to the side and was not always valued. It was rare to see a chief people officer or chief of human resources officer at the conference table.

Interestingly, you would never not have a chief financial officer at the table. Knowing that people are the greatest expense of the organization, why wouldn't you have a people expert guiding, coaching, and advising in the C-suite? And while many organizations have HR reporting through finance, stop and think about how much sense that makes. Yes, of course, HR has a large financial component. But it involves two totally different mind-sets—people and finance—two different talent sets. Many times the people are cut because of the financials and looked at as numbers versus an investment. I have scratched my head about that many times! Knowing the common approach to these areas of the business, I could see there was a disconnect.

I noticed that when organizations started to think differently about the value of a people strategy, the number of HR, people, and culture executives at the table increased. That was a great start. From there, I began to see that I needed to help these organizations focus on structuring the organization in accordance with their business strategy. Job descriptions were often written up without alignment to the organizational structure, setting the organization up for failure. How could they possibly get people who were great at what the organization needed them to be great at if job descriptions were reused, written hastily, or created by a single person rather than the whole involved team? Once I was able to clearly align the people strategy to the business strategy, we could all see quite demonstrably where the gaps were so we could fill them. Sometimes this involved hiring someone new to fill the job; other times, we could redistribute work among different team members. Either way, we now had very real data to guide us. This experience, which led to great results in organization after organization, led to the development of the Human Capital Optimization Model.

The Human Capital Optimization Model addresses the business foundation of an organization—in the form of culture, leadership, strategy, and brand—as well as the human side of an organization—in the form of how new employees are selected, hired, and managed and how existing employees are managed, developed, and promoted.

When organizations recognize that people are their greatest asset and treat them as such, the production enabled by the conscious deployment of their human capital has the potential to exceed the most optimistic projections. By being very clear on how their business foundation and people practices are implemented and by aligning them with each other, organizations can see substantial improvements in employee engagement, customer engagement, and profitability.

Figure 2.1: The Human Capital Optimization Model

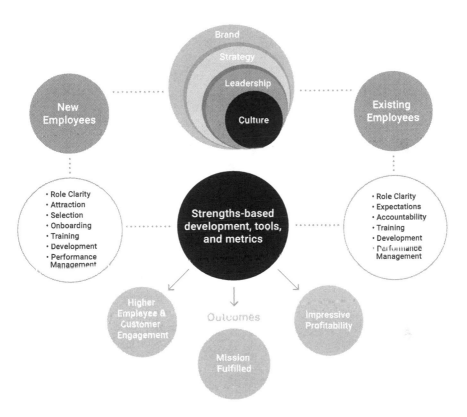

Let's look for a moment at both the business foundation and the people strategy of an organization to see why together they are so important. Each is necessary but not sufficient for success. On the business side, you can have the best culture, leadership, strategy, and brand in the world, but if you don't have good people to execute it, you won't achieve your desired results. On the human side, you can have the most talented employees in the right positions being managed by excellent managers, but if your company lacks strong leadership, strategy, branding, and a healthy culture, your employees will be unable to perform and produce desirable results. It will be impossible to successfully engage customers consistently over a period of time. When it comes to business strategy and people strategy, organizations need to have both. Most leaders understand this reality, whether implicitly or explicitly. Things get challenging when it comes to implementing and aligning the business foundation and people side of things. That's where the Human Capital Optimization Model comes in as a guide on where to focus when. Let's look at the business foundation first.

YOUR BUSINESS FOUNDATION: CULTURE, LEADERSHIP, STRATEGY, AND BRAND

Your people are your greatest asset, yes, but not in a vacuum: for their performance to be meaningful, it has to align with your business goals. Most leaders get this, yet there is often a breakdown somewhere on the business side of things that needs to be addressed. Before you dive into optimizing your human capital, I want you to be very clear on four characteristics defining your organization:

- Culture
- Leadership
- Strategy
- Brand

Culture

The Cambridge English Dictionary states that culture is "the way of life, especially the general customs and beliefs, of a particular group of people at a particular time."[4] When considering the culture of an organization, think of the culture as representing the organization's core, its essence. When you

> **Culture is the core of the organization.**

walk in the door, it's what you step into. When you come into contact with the organization or one of its representatives in any medium, you can feel or sense what the culture is like. Culture is about the human behavior that exists to help employees know what is acceptable or unacceptable, important or unimportant, and right or wrong at the organization. The deep heart of culture encompasses all learned and shared beliefs, assumptions, norms, and values. It extends to the attitudes, behavior, acceptable language, and dress of an organization's employees and leadership.

Culture and leadership are closely linked, and, like the chicken and the egg, it's not always clear which comes first. Leaders can foster culture or adapt it, but at the end of the day, culture is often bigger than the leader. Culture is the core of the organization. I find many times leaders who are new to the organization come in and change things but find that those changes they want to implement are not always accepted when they do not align with the existing culture. So, culture must be recognized and respected, because it is real. Then leaders and managers need to model behavior that aligns with the culture to perpetuate it, keeping it vital.

When an organization is looking to hire a new leader, manager, or employee, it is essential that the candidate is a fit to the culture or what the organization desires the culture to be, should changes be needed. When there is not a fit, other employees easily recognize the discrepancy and behave accordingly, and the new person literally feels like a fish out of water. However, when there is an unhealthy culture, things need to change, which is an issue in itself that leadership needs to take the time to tackle.

Leadership

Next, the Human Capital Optimization Model focuses on leadership, because leaders model the behaviors and show the way for others in the organization, whether they be on the leadership team, in management, or an employee. Leaders exist throughout the organization.In particular, it's the leaders who create the vision that employees align with and are going to get busy working to execute. Without an effective leader to create and communicate the vision, employees may not feel their work matters or is aligned to something bigger. They may simply go off and do their own thing, in their own way, causing distraction and inefficiency. Obviously, we want employees' efforts to be focused in the right areas.

Let's look at some quick examples related to vision. Elon Musk has such a powerful vision of a future in which technology is harnessed to solve problems and achieves incredible leaps in innovation that often push past current perceptions of what is possible that his companies—Tesla, SpaceX, and Solar City, among others—are redefining transportation, space travel, and energy production. This could never happen without his employees being similarly dedicated to and aligned with Musk's vision. Walt Disney had a vision for entertaining people that was so clear and captivating that his studios and theme parks, staffed not by employees but by cast members, are thriving and setting the standard in entertainment and customer service long after his death. A clear vision ensures that your employees know what they are striving for each day. It also enables you to structure jobs right and attract the people with the talents enabling them to execute that vision.

The leader needs to hold the spotlight on the mission of the organization, too, answering the question, "Why do we exist?" The mission is what the organization is set up to accomplish, the goal or ideal it is shooting for. Think of TOMS's pledge to make a donation to improve lives whenever a TOMS product is purchased,[5] Shopify's commitment to making it easier for people to engage in e-commerce,[6] and Dr. Bronner's dedication to philanthropy and progressive business practices.[7]

The leadership team plays a role in defining or refining the organizational mission, or the leader may simply put the mission into words by studying the heart of the organization and gleaning the mission from its market, operations, culture, and so on. Vision and mission can be created by the leader and embedded in the culture over time, or vision and mission may already be integrated in the culture and the leader can tease them out to align business strategy and human resource practices with them.

> **The wisest, most effective leaders are the ones who know themselves best and surround themselves with the rest.**

KNOW YOURSELF BEST,
SURROUND YOURSELF WITH THE REST

People always ask what makes the best leader. The best leaders are made of many talents. The wisest, most effective leaders are the ones who know themselves best and surround themselves with the rest. They know what they are good at and where they need other talented people to fill the gaps in their own talents. And here's the final element that's often missed: effective leaders then have the humility to listen to the people with complementary talents that they put into place to supplement their own areas of weakness.

That wasn't the case for Devon, an incredibly visionary leader in the insurance industry who could think outside of the box and sell people on his forward-thinking idea for a new approach to his business. He knew where he wanted to take his organization, but where his talents failed him were in the implementation of his vision and the strategy.

For example, he was unable to understand how to break down the whole project into the executable components that would need to be completed to achieve his vision. He had no sense of the time his team would require to get everything built and up to speed, and he struggled to build relationships with people. He was great at making promises about what would be accomplished, but he was not so great at setting up his employees in such a way and with adequate resources to meet those commitments. I will grant that Devon did have the sense to build a talented leadership team around him. Pride interfered, though, and Devon would neither take their advice nor give up control over any aspect of this operation. His ego was in the way.

Not surprisingly, the launch of Devon's new business idea, which came too soon and without enough support in place, was a bust. Devon, visionary that he was, had tapped into a rich vein of need in the insurance market, and customers came rolling in—too fast. Although the call center was set up to handle about five thousand calls a week, it instantly drew thirteen thousand individual calls. The employees did the best they could, but the call volume was overwhelming and the phone system kept crashing. Customers got frustrated that they couldn't get through and stopped calling.

Devon had his multimillion-dollar idea, but because he didn't have an adequate implementation strategy, his organization couldn't execute efficiently. He eventually made a go of it, but the road was much harder and longer than it had to be. His team and their teams lost confidence in his leadership, and the break-even point went beyond what investors had anticipated. The investors had to dump millions into the pie in the sky Idea to sustain the business. It takes humility to realize we can't be great at everything. When we enlist others who complement our weaknesses—and then give them the power to act—we get the best of all worlds and the results to go with it. In this case, vulnerability and humility would have gone a long way toward creating better outcomes, and it would have cost nothing in financial outlay.

Strategy

Next comes the strategy that's needed to support the vision and mission: the leader's how-to plan for executing (and selling) the mission and vision. Through strategy, leaders can determine, on the basis of the mission and vision, what they are going to sell, create, or provide.

- What are the revenue goals, net profit, and metrics of success?
- What are the key business goals that they will be executing in the next one, three, and five years?

- How does the organization perform consistently and get recurring business?

Leaders have to build a strategy around the organization's mission of why it exists and its vision for what is going to be accomplished. Without a clear organizational strategy that is then effectively communicated to everyone in the organization, the business units and employees don't really know what to focus on. What's more, the whole leadership team needs to be aligned and on the same page when it comes to strategy to avoid generating confusion within the organization. Dick Raines, the president of CARFAX, sums up the importance of communication well: "My No. 1 job is to make sure everyone in the company knows where we're going. That clarity is so important to people feeling like their jobs are meaningful."[8] Plus it makes sure everyone has the same map to get to where the company needs to go.

Firms in the same field can have completely different strategies, so different, in fact, that they can hardly be considered competitors. Take architecture firms. They're in the same business, yet they may focus on different markets and embrace different strategies. One of the architecture firms I work with specializes in education. They are the experts in building world-class schools and learning facilities. They have a ton of experience and plenty of ideas on how to build a learning space that maximizes the educational potential of kids and young adults. They could branch out to the corporate markets, but they don't. They've got their niche, their strategy is to specialize in the education market, and they're executing it with great success.

Another equally successful architectural firm works in about twelve different markets. They focus on corporate markets, churches, parks and recreational spaces, landscaping, senior housing, and health care facilities, among other projects. Their mission and vision are to work with clients to envision and create spaces that enrich life, work, play, and learning, using a highly collaborative and integrated process from start to finish; their different strategies are the different markets they enter to achieve their desired outcome.

Both of these firms have embraced strategies that have led them to success, but the key is that both of these firms had a strategy or strategies that their people could focus their energy and talents on, the talents of the employees aligned with what was needed to execute the strategies, and those strategies were clearly communicated to their people. By being in tune with their strategies and making sure their people are too, both firms are successful, even though they embrace different degrees of specialization.

get your hands on...

**STICKING WITH YOUR
STRATEGY—OR NOT**

Talking about having a strategy can be all well and good, but what happens when a lucrative business opportunity arises that doesn't fit your strategy? Do you forget about that idealistic mission statement you came up with at that meeting so long ago and instead focus on the fat fee that your organization could be earning? It's tempting, and I've seen leaders fall into this potential trap, diverting their organization away from its goals by taking a job that they think they should take but that doesn't fit into the vision of who they really are.

Notice that I said "potential" trap. Let's be realistic: Sometimes the opportunity is precisely that, an opportunity to go in a new and ultimately more successful direction. How do you make that choice? First, figure out whether this strategy change will align with who you are as an organization. If your mission is to have your organization do work that improves society while minimizing society's impact on the environment, does the specific product or service you're selling matter as much as fulfilling that mission? If you can change your strategy so that you can jump on a presented opportunity while still fulfilling your mission, a move like this may be worth serious consideration.

Second, what have we been talking about? Aligning your business foundation with your people strategy. So, it's time to get your mind on your people. Do you have the employees in place who can do this proposed work and the leaders capable of seeing it through? If your team has never before tackled a challenge along the lines of what your organization is now presented with, do you feel that they can make the changes you would be asking for while still remaining engaged with your workplace and mission? If you are confident that you have the right people, both leaders and employees, in place who can make this pivot with your organization, you are much better positioned to change your strategy and may be well-served if you do.

For example, We were working with a bank whose strategy was to expand by acquiring additional banks. Leadership was clear on the geographical locations they wanted to gain a foothold in and what kinds of banks they were looking to bring into their core business—those in markets with a demonstrated need for extended hours in the evenings and weekends.

All was going to plan, until the organization strayed from its strategy and started jumping on opportunities to acquire banks in sleepy towns where the demand for extended hours was small. Part of what this bank was good at was recruiting and hiring nontraditional bank tellers who were comfortable with the more modern notion of working on nights and weekends. Suddenly they were steering off course from their business strategy, which in turn would affect their people strategy. Would the same recruiting practices that had helped them build their bank in cosmopolitan markets serve them in sleepy towns with a different kind of human capital as well as customer? Fast forward to two years later. After following the Human Capital Optimization Model and evaluating their leadership and strategy, direction changed and a successful bank acquisition was accomplished. It was aligned to their core business and positively impacted their position in the market. Their business strategy and people strategy started to align, generating positive results.

Your mission can be revisited often to remind you who you are or who you intend to be. Know why your organization exists, then look at the new direction you're considering changing your strategy for. Does this new strategy align with who you are? Next, evaluate your human capital to make sure you have the right people to successfully move in your new direction while keeping your core business stable. If you want to be an organization with wide-ranging goods and services, go for it! That strategy is working just fine for Amazon and the Virgin Group. Just make sure that you've got your people in place to do it and everyone's on board with the new direction.

Brand

Next, the Human Capital Optimization Model focuses on brand, the image your organization projects into the world. Leaders know about brand; the challenge comes in the area of execution, whether that be consciously creating brand or managing brand—and, in our context, making sure that your people represent your brand internally and externally. Brand is the experience that people have with your organization. It's what people think about when they think of your organization; it's the unique taste and flavor that make you, you. Brand is how you represent yourself and what people think about when they think of you. Your goal is to emotionally attach people to the brand. When people like your brand, they come back to your business as repeat customers.

When I served as the Chief People Officer in a start-up health care company, the time came to choose what uniforms clinical employees would be wearing when they interacted with patients. This was a decision not just about company culture but about brand, as employees would be representing the organization to patients through the way they dressed. If we hadn't treated this as a branding opportunity, we might have simply had employees

> **Brand is how you represent yourself and what people think about when they think of you.**

dress in scrubs. Instead, mindful that scrubs could look oversized, sloppy, and too medical for our brand, we opted for a very different type of uniform instead: one that was more fitted, looked good on a wide range of body types, and came in a color that was warm and comforting to the patients. Patients would many times meet six or seven people in the clinic in different roles, so consistency in uniforms to enable the patients to recognize staff was important.

Uniforms or not, your employees represent your brand every day; let's have them act and think in accordance with your brand. We're not going for mind control but rather a sincere grounding of your people in your organization's vision, mission, and strategy, so they can walk the walk and talk the talk as they interact with each other and your customers.

Chick-fil-a has an incredibly strong and well-executed brand. The company is known for its faith-based philosophy, which means that there is an expectation for its employees to meet a higher-than-average standard when it comes to providing customers with a friendly, welcoming experience. And do their employees ever execute! You will hear "it's my pleasure" and "thank you" and will have employees calling you by your name when you go there—such welcoming language adds to an already positive experience (when you also consider the fast service and the tasty food). They strive for second-mile service, going above and beyond the already high standard they place on their brand.

Chick-fil-a sets very clear expectations for their employees, showing them exactly how to represent their company. That effort pays off in pleasant interactions with employees across restaurants. Customers know what to expect, and the brand brings them back to buy lunch (and breakfast, and dinner) again and again. To put it another way, the goal Chick-fil-a achieves and the one your organization should strive for is consistency in the representation of the brand.

When brand, strategy, leadership, and culture are all aligned with the people side of things, your employees know what they're working toward and you know you have your organization on the right path to achieving its goals. Table 2.1 shows how each of these four elements may look when functioning within a people-centered paradigm.

Table 2.1: Aligning Business Foundation and People Strategy Using the Human Capital Optimization Model

Business Foundation	People Strategy
Culture	Leadership respects the culture in which employees operate and makes strategic efforts to influence it when necessary.
Leadership	The leader creates and communicates the vision and mission so that employees understand how their work aligns to the mission and vision. The leadership team also models behavior that aligns with the culture the organization is striving for.
Strategy	The leadership team creates a strategy that aligns to achievement of the business goals and that employees use to execute their work aligning to the vision and mission. Employees need to understand the correlation between their role and the strategy.
Brand	The leadership team communicates and fosters brand within the organization strategy and culture so employees become brand ambassadors to colleagues and customers. Employees clearly understand how they represent the brand.

USING THE HUMAN ASPECT OF THE HUMAN CAPITAL OPTIMIZATION MODEL TO ACHIEVE CONSISTENT PERFORMANCE CONSISTENTLY

As we have seen, within the business aspect of the Human Capital Optimization Model, we have culture, leadership, strategy, and brand; on the people side, we have hiring new employees and managing the performance of existing employees. The human aspect of the model provides organizations with a strategic approach to filling positions with the right people to execute organizational mission, vision, and strategy—and then managing them well. It's about getting the right people on the bus, sitting them in the right seats, and finding the right bus driver to give them attention and grow them.

This aspect of the Human Capital Optimization Model will provide you with the tools you need to get the very best out of your employees, maximizing your in-house talent. That being said, as much as the ideal is to maximize employees' talents, I find that most leaders would be happy with simply achieving consistent positive performance from their employees, day after day, because from that consistency comes reliability and steady results. I call this *consistent performance consistently.*

The reason that the Human Capital Optimization Model is so good at fostering consistent performance and maximizing talent is because it provides tools to ensure that people are doing jobs that they are great at and that these jobs have been designed in sync with the organizational mission, vision, and strategy. That's the left side of the model (see Figure 2.1 earlier in the chapter). Equally important, the right side of the model (see Figure 2.1) includes a focus on getting management right: putting the right people in management roles and providing them with the tools they need to manage employees effectively, from setting expectations and providing feedback to ensuring accountability. Oftentimes, people don't leave companies, they leave managers, so getting the right management team in place can help to address turnover issues and maintain consistent employee performance.

When thinking about aligning the people strategy of your organization with the business strategy, you want to be aware of the following:

- Right fit
- Strengths-based management

When you have hired the right person for the job, that's right fit. The person in the role has the talents, skills, knowledge, experience, and values to do the job well and that person is a cultural fit—a round peg in a round hole.

There's another important element of right fit—being clear, before hiring, on what the job really needs to be to accomplish the work in that role that aligns to the organizational goals. Once you know what the role should entail to lead to desired business results, you are set up to attract and hire the right candidate. It's common sense that the job description and the hire should match, and yet most organizations are failing to adequately define job roles before filling them. Job descriptions exist, but these descriptions tend to miss the mark, setting employers up for failure before the interviewing process has even begun. Many times, when someone leaves an organization, the employee is replaced without anyone taking the time to evaluate the role to see if the role addresses key and current needs of the

> **Most leaders would be happy with simply achieving consistent positive performance from their employees, day after day, because from that consistency comes reliability and steady results. I call this *consistent performance consistently.***

organization. (Chapters 4 and 5 provide tips and tools for conducting the hiring and selection process well.)

So you found a great employee who is a perfect fit for the role. Hold on a minute: The best newly hired employee in the world can't function well with a poor manager. This is where effective management comes in: setting clear expectations, delegating work, holding people accountable, giving consistent feedback and knocking barriers out of the way for people.

Good managers have the talent to coach, guide, encourage, and direct people and to have tough conversations. That means that we should be putting individuals who know how to coach, guide, direct, delegate, hold people accountable, and so on into management roles. They need to have the talent to be a manager, which is one of the reasons I refer to it as strengths-based management. Sounds evident, and yet in organizations today, we tend to promote people because they are really good individual performers in their specialty, not because they evidence strong management skills and talents.

The talent of a superstar individual performer and the talent of a great manager are often different. Sam might be really good at programming, so we think it makes sense for him to manage the group, but if he lacks key management skills like relationship building and effective communication, all the programming skills in the world aren't going to set him up for success as a manager.

As with hiring new employees, we need to be sure that the job descriptions for any management roles are written accurately. Does the manager of the IT group really need incredible programming skills? If so, Sam's still in the running for the job. Where are they to spend most of their time in the role? That needs to be a key focus in selecting the right manager. Does the manager need to be able to lead meetings, manage projects to completion, and provide regular employee feedback? If so, let's make sure Sam's got the talent to fulfill these roles before promoting him into the role.

> **As managers set expectations, create accountability, measure employee performance, and give feedback, it's all done within the context of knowing what the employees do best.**

At its core, management consists of many responsibilities, but the two key types of responsibilities are people management and project management. How much time a manager needs to spend on projects or people depends on the specific position, and that's something to define and hire for when the position is created. Given that many individual performers who end up being a manager did not intend to be one, it's natural enough that many are more comfortable with managing projects than people. People are complicated! They have feelings, they have good days and bad days, and sometimes they don't get along. They need feedback and attention. There's no diagnostic program to run to see what's going wrong, and a proposed fix may work with one person and not another.

This discomfort with the people side of things, paired with the desire to execute and recreate past project successes, can lead to a manager tackling projects personally rather than delegating the work to others on the team. This is why it is essential to maintain role clarity for your managers by writing a specific job role description and holding the manager accountable for the expectations of the position. (Chapter 7 provides guidance on how to hire and develop managers with the talent and tools to elicit world-class performance from their people.)

Strengths-based management also involves managing employees using a strengths-based development approach. As managers set expectations, create accountability, measure employee performance, and give feedback, it's all done within the context of knowing what the employees do best, harnessing their talents, and turning them into strengths by adding skills, knowledge, and experience. It's essential that the manager know an employee's strengths from the start by using reputable assessments, such as the Clifton StrengthsFinder, DiSC, the Myers-Briggs Type Indicator, or Emergentics.

With this knowledge in hand, the manager can know how to best set the individual up for success, set realistic expectations, hold the employee accountable for that which he or she is capable of, and understand performance results, which should correlate with employee strengths. With my background from Gallup in StrengthsFinder, my team and I are strongly versed in the strengths approach and are partners in helping managers create

more to get your mind on...

HOW TO PROMOTE SUPERSTAR PERFORMERS WHO HIT THE MANAGEMENT GLASS CEILING

There comes a point in a lot of people's careers, after they've put in a chunk of time with an organization and achieved some success, when they are often expected to be applying for or promoted to a management position. Getting ahead at an organization—and receiving the raise that goes with it—means, to many people, becoming a manager. Some do just that, with varying degrees of success in the new position. But what do you do with those employees who want more recognition and responsibility and the opportunity to bring home a bigger paycheck but who do not have the management talent profile or are not passionate about investing in and developing people? For more information on this challenging but common situation, go to www.loristohs.com/getyourmindon.

a scorecard of their team members' strengths so they can manage with great success. (Chapter 8 provides a comprehensive look at how to manage performance in a way that optimizes your human capital, making for engaged and high-performing employees.)

The sum result of employing right fit and strengths-based management is strengths-based engagement. New employees and existing employees perform at their best, and consistently, because they are in roles that play to their strengths. Managers know how to bring out the best in team members, so both managers and employees shine. Ultimately, all of these efforts are ideally aligned with organizational culture, leadership, strategy, and brand. It's a powerful combination that allows organizations to function at their highest potential (see Figure 2.2.).

Figure 2.2: Human Capital Optimization Model Close-Up: Culture, Leadership, Strategy, and Brand

CONCLUSION: PEOPLE IMPACT YOUR BOTTOM LINE

Human resource issues have traditionally been seen as the "soft stuff" in business that have less impact on the bottom line than "harder" or more substantive areas like product development, sales, operations, finance, and IT. In truth, people issues are really the hard stuff. When we start to identify the large number of employees who are being assigned work that they aren't good at and managers who weaken departments because they have no business running teams, it becomes more clear how people have a huge impact on the bottom line. All of these issues affect the outcomes businesses are working to achieve.

The Human Capital Movement calls leaders to put a much higher value on their people strategy than they are currently, and the Human Capital Optimization Model provides the structure to align the people strategy with the business foundation. When your payroll is millions of dollars, it just makes sense to invest in your people strategy to make sure you get the most out of your investment. Instead of cutting payroll to increase profitability, how about understanding payroll and understanding how much waste in the organization really exists?

To put things in perspective: You would never not have a chief financial officer at the leadership table of a large organization, yet you will rarely find a chief people officer. As the Human Capital Movement takes hold in a widespread fashion, we may just start to see that change.

3

THE WHOLE PERSON MODEL

A Comprehensive Approach to Selection and Performance

When driving through a new city, what do you typically think about? Do you keep an eye out for trendy restaurants? Check out the architecture? Admire the green spaces? As a human capital consultant and someone whose passion revolves around people in the workplace, when I drive through a new city, I often gaze at the office buildings as I pass by and wonder, "What's it like to work there? What's going on in that organization? How are the employees feeling? Do they love their work? Hate it? Do they have great managers and a great leadership team? What does the culture look like, feel like, inside?" I'm pretty sure not everybody asks these questions, but given my interests and the nature of my work, I do!

Because of my professional background and talent, when I walk into an organization, I can typically sense quite quickly what it's like to work there: whether employees are engaged, awake, and empowered to do what they need to do with a sense of freedom or instead if it's a fear-based environment that has caused people to devolve and shut down. You may be able to feel the level of engagement at an organization, too, but most people are not able to put their finger on exactly what is driving the environment to be what it is. They can't see the underbelly of what's really the cause of engagement or of disengagement. It's just a sense, a feel, and a connection of the multifaceted components making up an organization.

Even so, we can all relate to questions like the following: Why are some people really good at what they do? Why are some people not so good at what they do? Why do you have some people at work who are knocking it out of the park and consistently performing and some people who are just making it through the day, coming in to make the widgets and going home as soon as the quitting bell rings? Maybe the most important question of all is, what is the reason that some employees are engaged and others are not?

A key answer to that question is *fit*: the degree to which an employee's talents, skills, knowledge, and experience make the employee well suited for a particular job and organization (as well as the employee's team and manager, but more on that later in the chapter). When I consult with organizations to help them improve any number of business issues—be it workplace conflict, low performance, high turnover, or employee disengagement—I find the root cause of many of these problems is that organizations don't have the right people in the right roles. They are having problems with fit.

Problems with fit can be identified early, when hiring someone new for the job or when promoting individuals into new positions (the left side of the Human Capital Optimization Model, explained in chapter 2). Clearly, it

> *fit*: the degree to which an employee's talents, skills, knowledge, and experience make the employee well suited for a particular job and organization

is much better to discover fit issues before you put someone into a role than after you've built a department or an initiative around that person!

I have developed the Whole Person Model to help organizations improve their successes in the area of hiring and selecting through fit, so they are able to get fit right from the start. When individuals are put into roles and cultures for which they have a good fit, they thrive, they stay engaged, and they remain awake! And, of course, that is what we want. According to Gallup's 2016 Q[12] Meta-Analysis, businesses scoring in the top quartile on employee engagement measures are 20 percent more productive and 21 percent more profitable than businesses scoring in the bottom quartile.[1] Sounds appealing, right? The Whole Person Model can be used to help you achieve great fit between your people and their job roles so that they remain engaged and awake, with all the good outcomes that those states bring.

NEED EMPLOYEE FIT? GET FOCUSED

When I work with an organization and we drill down into the challenges they are having, we often discover that they are really dealing with a problem of fit between an individual and the role in which that individual is employed. For example, what looks like a marketing problem has to do with the director of marketing rather than one specific marketing campaign; what looks like a technology challenge originates back to the person who led the team to implement it rather than the new tech per se.

If you take only one thing of practical use from this book, let it be an awareness of the importance of looking at the people side of any problem you may be facing. Wherever the problem lies, I encourage you to trace it back to the people involved and then ask the question, "Are these people the right fit for their role?" The answer will almost always provide useful guidance.

Even when you recognize that fit is important, it can still be a challenging task to get the right people in the right roles. This can occur for a number of reasons:

- Job descriptions for new openings are made with the wrong criteria in mind.
- People are hired without proper assessments of their talent. When assessments are completed, is the data being interpreted specifically for the role?

- Internal candidates are promoted to management roles because they are star performers in their field, but they don't have the appropriate skills and talents to manage a department.

The Whole Person Model highlights the five key areas that employers will benefit from considering when assessing whether a candidate is the right fit for a new job or an internal promotion: (a) talent, (b) skills, (c) knowledge, (d) experience, and (e) values. The outer ring representing fit also serves as a reminder that although the candidate's characteristics are important, the way the employee will fit in the new job environment also must be considered when hiring.

Figure 3.1: The Whole Person Model

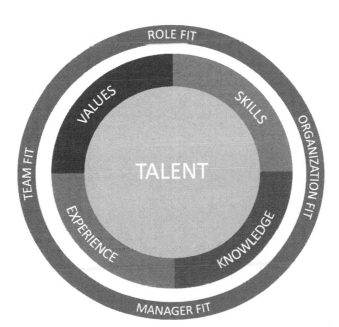

Think of the central circle in the Whole Person Model as representing your employee or potential employee, and within this circle is the talent this person has to offer—the core of "who they are." The ring around the core represents the fit of the employee with the role, organization, manager, and team. The five areas in the core circle of the model can also explain why an existing employee is performing well versus performing below expectations. The five elements are defined as follows.

1.   *Talent* is who we are. It's innate—the recurring patterns of thought, feeling, or behavior productively applied. It all starts at the core. We show up as who we were made to be from birth. This is the nature component—our genetics and our personality. At the core, talents represent the person. Then, over time, we grow up and learn skills.

2.   *Skills* are what we have been taught, from crawling to walking to running to reading. With practice, we acquire and enhance our skills and learn to apply them in new ways, such as in executing the steps of a process (e.g., bookkeeping, computer programming, writing a press release). In the early years, the acquisition of knowledge is a big part of life.

3.   *Knowledge* is what we know. This is the information learned through schooling, reading, learning, and listening. We then gain experience.

4.   *Experience* is what we've done. We've gained experience by simply jumping in and doing things and hopefully gaining

wisdom along the way. We have learned through trials and tribulations.

5. *Values*, our standards and beliefs, are a part of who we are and the life priorities placed upon us while growing up. They represent what standards and beliefs are important to us.

Fit is a feeling. It is what happens when the talent, skills, knowledge, experience, and values a job candidate brings to the table align with the job role, organization, manager, and team. When all are synchronous, engagement can be off the charts! Yet when they don't, watch out for disengagement and fireworks of the decidedly unpleasant kind. The result can be a dispirited employee for whom work is unending drudgery, each day serving as a soul-killing slog to quitting time. That's not good for anyone.

Let's look at each of these elements in turn.

Skills are teachable. A person can learn how to use Power-Point, drive a car, or trouble-shoot standard billing problems on the phone with a customer. Skills are convenient for your job candidates to have, but skills can often be supplied by you in the form of classes, tutoring, or mentoring if you have someone who is otherwise a great fit for the role you're hiring for. This is why skills make up only a part of the Whole Person Model. The skill level cannot be world class without the talent. When natural talent exists, it's the game changer that leads to world-class performance.

Knowledge is learning, acquired through school, reading, and listening, and is often exemplified by degrees and certifications.

A strong base of knowledge readies a person to learn applications of that knowledge to an industry, a product, or an expertise; a knowledgeable person can also get off to a faster start on the job if no remedial learning is required. Again, though, training is something that you could potentially supply for the candidate who is a good fit in other ways for the job you are hiring for but lacks some of the necessary knowledge.

Experience is what you have done, having lived and practiced in a role before. Has your candidate for the marketing team held a position in marketing before? If you are a technology company, are you seeking candidates with prior time at tech firms? Has your new hire for human resources spent time doing the core work you are expecting of her at a previous place of employment? Experience is often the ingredient we seek when hiring someone new for the role. Having prior experience is helpful, but where employers sometimes get tripped up is in overemphasizing the importance of experience in a given industry or role without also considering how that experience stacks against a person's innate talents. Just because a person has done the work doesn't mean he is the best at it.

Think of it this way. Would you rather hire

- someone who has three years' experience in accounting but was disengaged and miserable the entire time because she is a creative person who has trouble sitting at a computer managing budgets and spreadsheets but it's just what she has done?

OR

- someone who easily sees patterns in numbers, finds it relaxing to sit at his desk, and is structured and detail oriented but who has never worked in an accounting department and does not know how to use the advanced features of Excel?

The short-term view has many of us quickly going for the candidate who has accounting experience on her résumé as if that's the Easy Button. What I am now challenging you to do with your human capital consciousness turned on is to look deeper and consider a better long-term play, which is to find out who has the talent for the accounting role you are seeking. You can always teach accounting skills and knowledge; and experience can be gained. Talent for instantly seeing the patterns of numbers in the budgets and or quickly catching errors others didn't see in balance statements? A person either does or does not have it.

With your human capital consciousness in tune, you will be able to see from the very start those candidates with red flags signaling future disengagement and role failure due to lack of talent versus those who have a golden halo circling their head, signaling it's the talented, right potential super star with true fit for the role. That kind of second sight will not only relieve you and your organization of otherwise unforeseen snags down the road when the person with the wrong fit for the job goes zombie,[2] but it will give you an edge over your competitors who do not have the same sharpened human capital consciousness as you possess.

As for values, these often reflect how we were raised—our nurturing and our environment—influencing how we behave and our sense of how things should be. A child who was not a born organizer may end up being quite meticulous once grown because Mom spent hours making sure everything was just so and holding her children to the same standard. A football player may never cuss, no matter what he hears in the locker room, because his father told him that the men in their family would never lower themselves to speak like that. If the reason someone gives for their behavior is, "That's the way I was brought up," then that behavior reflects the values that he or she grew up believing in. It's the ethics in accordance to which someone acts, even though that behavior may not be entirely natural to him or her. People are different, personalities are different, and the way we respond to things is different. This is nature. How we were raised—the rules, the guidelines—influence us. This is nurture. Maybe I want to do something one way, but I wasn't raised to do things that way, so I don't.

> The short-term view has many of us going for the candidate who has experience on her résumé as if that's the Easy Button. What I am now challenging you to do with your human capital consciousness turned on is to look deeper and consider a better long-term play, which is to find out who has the talent for the role.

How do you keep the values piece in mind when hiring? Try to determine whether the candidate's values align with your organization's values. Here's the thing: although values are a conditioned characteristic (that is, values aren't innate the way that talents are), they also aren't likely to change, and if they do change, they don't change much, usually based on the season of life. Values are the product of the nurture part of nature versus nurture, and the programming runs deep.

Take, for example, a teacher I met at a nonprofit organization for children. This teacher was very capable, but he was also extremely rigid, a disciplinarian, and overall very authoritative. In some environments—a military academy comes to mind—this sort of approach to teaching would have been fine. However, this approach to interacting with children was too much for the vulnerable children this nonprofit served. The last thing the kids needed was to have someone to rebel against! His values were really extreme—he was not a good fit for the environment. Use your judgment when it comes to vetting values and their cohesion with the values of your organization. If a fit of values is not there at the beginning of the collaboration, then don't think you can change that.

ZEROING IN ON TALENT

When employers fill positions, they often focus on seeking individuals with the right skills, knowledge, and experience. This is the information filling the résumé that they see in front of them. Yet, a big piece of that job candidate is missing from the résumé:

who the person is beyond his skills, knowledge, and experience. What is missing is that person's values and, more important, his talent. Talent—the largest component of a person—is often overlooked. What a shame! Résumés don't tend to contain talents—things like strategic thinking, responsibility, and an analytical approach. A job title may occasionally include such terms, but just because someone served as a *strategic marketing director* doesn't mean that that person has strategic thinking as a natural talent.

As I've said already, talents are innate. They're natural abilities. They can't be taught. Talent is who we are. Some people can walk into a room where two people are arguing and defuse the tense situation with a few well-placed words and observations; suddenly everyone's laughing and the problem has been resolved. Some people can pick up a piece of tech and figure out how it works (and how to use it in ways even the inventor hasn't thought of) by playing with it for a short period of time.

For those who have discovered their talents, the well of talents is bottomless; some people use theirs all the time, and some people don't even realize they have them. At the same time, these characteristics are invaluable to identify and hire for if you want the best fit and the most engaged employees. After all, which job would most people prefer to work in and bring their best to every day: the one they have skills, knowledge, and experience for yet still feel awkward and out of their comfort zone, or the one that comes to them so naturally that it feels like it was made with them in mind? To gain more insight into talents, take a look at some examples:

- Has a way with words
- Sees patterns of data quickly
- Is in tune to others' emotions
- Able to see the future
- Able to build bridges between the two sides of a conflict
- Understands the uniqueness of others
- Connects easily with people
- Thinks of many options for the solution
- Excellent at organization
- Gets things started
- Sees the steps naturally to gets things done
- Able to manage multiple projects at one time
- Finds the problem before others know it exists
- Sorts through layers of issues and sees the solution

When I emphasize the importance of talents, this is not to shortchange the value of skills, knowledge, and experience. These are all important, but bear in mind that they each make up only part of what you should be looking for in a job candidate, while talent makes up much more. Talent is ability a candidate was born with—it's something your candidate either has or doesn't have. If you've ever traveled to remote islands (or if you've seen the movie *Six Days, Seven Nights*), you may have heard the saying, "If you didn't bring it here, you're not going to find it here." That's the way it is with talent: If it isn't there to begin with, it's not going to spontaneously develop. If a certain talent is required for the job, your candidate better have it! Skills, knowledge, and experience can be provided or added to—you can help your candidate acquire these things, even if they don't arrive in your workplace with them.

According to an article written by Bain & Company employees Michael Mankins, Alan Bird, and James Root and published in *Harvard Business Review*, "In fields that involve repetitive, transactional tasks, top performers [employees with talent] are typically two or three times as productive as others. . . . In highly specialized or creative work, the differential is likely to be a factor of six or more."[3] They note as more concrete examples that the best software developer at Apple has nine times the productivity of an average developer employed by another organization, and an average retail salesperson is outsold by a factor of eight by a top Nordstrom sales associate.[4]

TAPPING INTO TALENT

Does talent really matter? Sometimes words are used interchangeably, so I want to be clear on what I mean when I am talking about talent. *Talent* is naturally recurring patterns of thought, feeling, or behavior, productively applied. Talent is natural. It's easy. It's when you are in the flow and it happens over and over again, consistently. Consistency is huge with talent. For organizations to be successful, we need consistency.

Think of something that is natural for you. If you are naturally strategic, you are always thinking of multiple solutions for your problems. You don't wake up and say "Hmm, I think I am going to think of lots of different options." That's just where you live. You have a dominant talent, which is the natural state of who you are.

Many times people will say, "Well, it's not my favorite thing, but I can do it." Well, that sounds convincing, doesn't it? But if I am having a pre-op consultation with a surgeon, I don't want him, when I ask him about doing the procedure, to fiddle with his pen while looking away from me and saying, "I can do it, but . . ." I want him to look me in the eye; state that he is ready, willing, and able to do it (but not too eagerly—this is surgery I'm talking about!); and have a demonstrated track record of being consistent at doing it well all of the time! If you have children, you want to have the best teacher in the classroom, not one who shows up and is good part of the time. Excellence exists in talent, consistently. We are all human and not perfect, but I think you get the point. Talent is something you do all day, every day, without even thinking about it.

I am working with an executive right now who is struggling with this concept. I always say to him, "You can't teach touch," because you can't. "You can't teach competitiveness, you can't teach empathy, and you can't teach strategic thinking. You can't teach people to think futuristically or think analytically or see patterns of data." Those are things that cannot be taught. They are just part of the natural wiring of a human being. My client has heard me explain this concept multiple times, and yet he is still holding on to this idea that with the right coaching, certain employees will be able to significantly improve their performance even though they lack talent for their roles.

My team has been asking the executive, "How much time

do you really want to spend on this?" because we know from many other projects how futile a task it can be to get someone to perform in areas where they lack the necessary talent. Sure, you want to give people an opportunity to be aware of an area of weakness and correct it, but if it's not their natural wiring, no amount of teaching or coaching will ever make them a world-class performer consistently.

You might be thinking, "What if someone has the talent but it's not applied?" That is a great question. Talent is raw. Once you take the core talent and add skills, knowledge, experience, and values, then it moves it to the next level and becomes a strength! If you're also thinking, "What if someone has a talent but doesn't like using it?" you're right, that's a concern, too. Superhero movies explore this theme a lot—for example, Hulk, the Thing of the Fantastic Four, and Diablo of the Suicide Squad all actively fought their talents throughout their respective films before embracing them heroically by the end. (May their issues never be the issues you are dealing with in the workplace, though!)

For an example in the real-life work world, I am reminded of the person on your team you always turn to, to mediate between arguing parties. She may have discovered her talent for calming down a roomful of individuals who don't agree because of a troubled domestic situation while growing up. Could you blame her for not wanting to use that talent, innate and strong though it may be? With your reluctant mediator or anyone who does not want to employ a talent any more than necessary, make sure you engage in a dialogue about what they're willing to do and contribute, and consider limiting the amount of time you ask that person to use that talent.

Finally, do not mistake passion for talent. A person may be very enthusiastic in conversation about a topic or a process, but that doesn't mean that the person has any natural talent in the area he or she loves. Don't we all know that techie wannabe who can tell you everything about his latest gadget but can't make it actually work? Or that self-proclaimed salesperson who has yet to close a deal? If possible, find a place to channel that employee's passion. Rather than putting your almost-techie in IT, how about having him write a column for the organizational newsletter on applications for the latest tech in your industry? And the salesperson may have better luck in putting the right people together with the right projects. With her interest in developing people, she just might be management material (see chapters 7 and 8 for more on what to look for in managers).

Overlook talent when hiring at your own risk. Bill, an area sales manager in Boston who led a team of medical device sales reps, had an opening for a sales rep in one of his territories. We had a hiring process in place for the company, so he called me to let me know he had a candidate for the opening that he was over-the-top excited about, Barry. Barry had experience with a competitor, and Bill really liked Barry. Bill knew him from the industry and had spent time with him socially, so thought he was a good guy. Well, anyone who knows me knows I will say that there are a lot of "good guys" or "nice people" out there, but that doesn't mean they are the right one for the job. Yet Bill was sure that this candidate was perfect.

After I completed the assessment with Barry, I could see that Barry brought a lot to the table in general, but he had some significant talent gaps for this particular position. He was a doer and built relationships, but he was not conceptual and was not able to problem solve in the moment, which was needed in this case. The role Bill needed to fill worked with surgeons in the surgery room and required a person to think quickly and respond on a dime with alternative solutions when problems arose.

As I always leave the final decision to the manager, when I brought my assessment of Barry to him, Bill said, "OK, I think I can manage that. I will spend time with him in the field teaching him this." I told Bill that talents like problem solving and conceptual thinking are not really teachable. I reminded him that he had nine other reps scattered across the northeast that he had to continue managing as well. Bill waved me off and made the hire.

Three months later, Bill called and said, "You were right." Although I never say "I told you so," I appreciated the feedback. Bill reported, "Exactly what you told me would happen, happened. I spent all this time in person with him, teaching, and he still can't do the job on his own." Well, good learning for Bill to recognize that the talent couldn't be taught. If it isn't in, you can't put it in. If it is in, you can pull it out, grow, and develop it! That's where success comes from. That's where world-class performance exists. Easily.

On the positive side, another client, Catrina, caught herself being tempted to hire someone that she really liked due to her skills and expertise after we had a discussion on the candidate's talent and realized she lacked what she needed for the role. Catrina was hiring for a procurement role and although the applicant had many years of experience, she didn't have the talent that would align to this role for their organization. Catrina realized it was better to wait to find the right one—Ms. Right rather than Ms. Right Now. She took her time before hiring a different candidate, Candace, who is now flourishing and producing consistently at a high level, not only doing the work but creating new processes and ways of doing the work more efficiently and effectively.

If you hire someone who interviews really well but that person doesn't work out in the role, the hire may not have had the right talent for the job. The same goes for existing employees who aren't performing well. (A mismatch in values, poor management, and a bad cultural fit with the team or organization can also be culprits, but many times talent is the missing piece.)

Once you get a clear read on the talents of your employees and potential hires, you can avoid similarly faulty expectations for them, being sure to match their talents up with the jobs where they can use them. Then, when you take the next step and put a candidate's skills, knowledge, experience, talents, and values together, you will discover that person's *strengths*, and you are truly on the right path to matching the right person with the right job.

> **Once you get a clear read on the talents of your employees and potential hires, you can avoid faulty expectations for them, being sure to match their talents up with the jobs where they can use them.**

What are strengths? We've already seen how talents are innate and how skills, knowledge, experience, and values are developed as a person grows, learns, and undertakes work in the world. When we put this all together and someone starts with a talent and applies skills, knowledge, experience, and values to it—exercising and exploring that talent, harnessing it and learning to use it—that talent is brought to a productive level, transforming it into a strength. A strength is a talent elevated to realize its full potential, and it's a thing to behold!

Keep in mind that a strength needs to be used to be fully developed. If you have a talent but never use it, that talent benefits no one, and it doesn't achieve the level of strength. Yet imagine if you could be the one to enable a person to use her strengths in the workplace—that means engagement for the person and an optimally done job for your organization. It's a win–win that comes from applying the Whole Person Model and being in tune to your human capital consciousness when hiring and promoting.

get your hands on...

FITTING THE RIGHT PEOPLE
IN THE RIGHT JOBS

There are two particularly important aspects to making sure you match your people with the right jobs. First, you need to make sure you have a really good job description that captures not just needed skills, knowledge, and experience but also the talents required for the job. This is how you will recognize the right person for the job. This is common sense, yes, but it is a strategy often missed by employers. Second, you need to understand what a job candidate's talents are before placing that person in a particular new job, not just what her skills, knowledge, experience, and values are. With this approach, you can fit the employee and the job role together like two matching puzzle pieces.

Step 1: Creating a Talent-Based Job Description

Let's look at the first part of finding the right person for the job: job descriptions. When I am meeting with executives for the first time to help them understand how my consulting firm can help them, they will often tell me that to address some of their existing problems, they need to hire to fill a new role. When I stand at the whiteboard and ask them to define the role, they'll say something like, "Well, we need somebody who knows how to work with our software, and we need someone with this degree, and we need someone with five years of experience in running these kinds of projects."

"Great," I'll say and write all that up on the board, recognizing that they have just listed off skills, knowledge, and experience. I'm thinking, *where's the talent?* To get at that component of the Whole Person Model, I ask the team to then describe somebody they already have in that role at the organization who they want more of.

"Who is your best in this role? Describe to me that person," I will say. Guess what they describe to me? A list of talents! If they're picking a salesperson, they're saying, "I want someone who's competitive, I want someone who's great at relationships, I want someone with drive, I want someone who's strategic, I want this, I want that." When I'm listing all of these behaviors that they're describing—every time!—at least 90 percent of what I put on the board is in the talent category. All of a sudden there is a big "aha." Talent is essential!

Rich, a successful, experienced, business leader was a client working with us. He had chosen new employees based on skills and experience for years. We walked through this activity, and he realized he had a gap of talent in the past. The picture became very clear why that was occurring.

The problem is that most hiring processes do not include a talent component; therefore, employers are missing a huge tool for ensuring a good fit of the employee to the job, full engagement, and high performance. If you want to hire the right talent, be sure to take the time to brainstorm the true talents that are needed for the job! (See chapter 4 for more guidance on how to write a talent-based job profile.)

Step 2: Identifying a Candidate's Talents

Now let's look at the second part of finding the right person for the job: identifying a person's talents before placing or promoting him or her into the new job or role. Be wary of the faulty résumé! Just like employers who are focused on skills, knowledge, and experience, most job candidates are also focused on these three things, and they do not showcase their talents on their résumés or CVs.

If you look at most people's résumés, they don't include anything about how they can use their talent in a given role. You know how long this candidate was working for a hometown newspaper, but you don't know how he strategized a new advertising package that pulled in more advertising dollars while it also boosted circulation. You can see that your candidate graduated from Princeton, but you don't realize that she was so empathetic that she talked multiple students in her dorm out of dropping out and saved more than a few couples' relationships. She was a natural counselor who understood people well.

I've looked at thousands of résumés, and I can see that job candidates consistently miss the talent piece. Yet, at the end of the day, if I'm an employer, talent is really what I should be basing my choice of an employee on: whether that person's talents fit with the needs of the particular job role. If they have skills, knowledge, and experience, that's even better, but talent is a top priority because it cannot be taught once on the job.

Remember, you're not just looking for a good person to hire: you're looking for the right person to do the specific job you are hiring for who is a good fit with the job, manager, team, and organization. That means that you need to take a good, long look at both the job candidate and the job description. If the skills, knowledge, experience, values, and talents of the job candidate—if that person's strengths—do not match the requirements of the job you are hiring for, keep on looking. As your grandmother might have said, "There are plenty more fish in the sea." The right match is out there; you just have to find it. By holding out for the right match, you can save yourself and your organization many headaches down the road.

GET FIT ON FOUR LEVELS

When using the Whole Person Model, as we have seen, we need to find fit between the employee and the job role. This is a key component of engagement, as this is where the work is being done and where the employee spends most of his time. But fit does not stop there. We also need the right fit with the manager, the team, and the organization. Have you ever had someone who was a great performer of the work, but that same individual caused a lot of drama in the organization? Or think of a time when you knew that person had to go, but this individual was a top performer and you didn't want to get rid of him or her. Yet, the instant you did, wow, the dynamics of the team changed, engagement increased, and you and your team had a lot more time and energy on your hands. That's it. Sometimes a person doesn't fit.

Fit is a feeling. You know if something fits, the same way you can recognize the right fit in your clothes. You don't have to wonder whether your jeans are too tight—you just know! With people, fit is "what works." I recently had a conversation with a client whose company just had to let go of the CEO, which, as you can imagine, was a big deal; transitions and executive searches are a time of turmoil for an organization. During the conversation, my client commented, "Oh, I knew right away he wasn't a fit, right from the beginning." Wasn't that telling? But we want to try to give people a chance.

I want to give people a chance as well, but I want to help companies think first, before we bring people through the door, what criteria to consider for the role and the fit. And if an employee is on payroll and it's not working, we need to know how we can evaluate what is working and what is not. Imagine the trouble this company could have avoided had this executive's instinct been expressed and heeded. The upheaval executive transition brings not only affects that CEO and his life, but the time and energy in an organization that is spent on distraction, change, and drama.

When I look at fit, fit has four components. The first is *fit for the role*, which we have already discussed in detail. What is the role? Does the role match the person's skills, knowledge, expertise, talents, and values? If I've got the person on one hand and the job on the other hand and I put them together, the two hands more or less interlock equally. If only a few areas align, we are not going to see consistent performance. This is why it's critical to outline not only the role but also the percentage of time the person will be doing what functions in that role. We have a tendency to see the things we like about that person, but then we don't align that to how much time they will be doing that work versus everything else required in the role.

Figure 3.2: The Fit Model

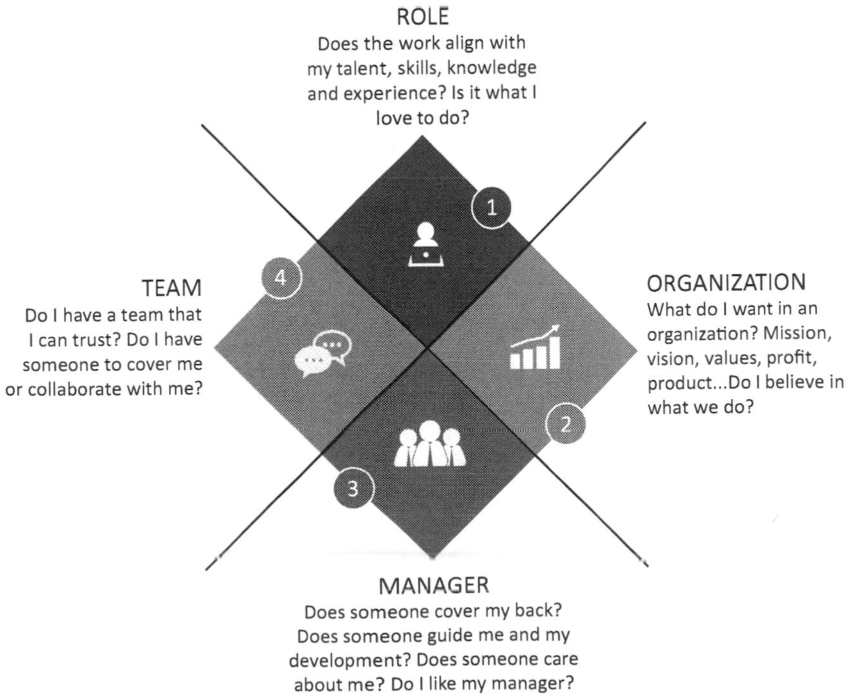

ROLE
Does the work align with
my talent, skills, knowledge
and experience? Is it what I
love to do?

TEAM
Do I have a team that
I can trust? Do I have
someone to cover me
or collaborate with me?

ORGANIZATION
What do I want in an
organization? Mission,
vision, values, profit,
product...Do I believe in
what we do?

MANAGER
Does someone cover my back?
Does someone guide me and my
development? Does someone care
about me? Do I like my manager?

The second category is a *fit for the organization*, when the job candidate, new hire, or existing employee suits the organization and vice versa. It involves questions like, "Is the person a fit for our organization and what we stand for? Can the person do well in an organization our size? Will this person represent us and align to our mission and values? Is the person conscious of what he or she is looking for in an employer and does it match who we are?" Alignment between organization and employee is needed in many different categories, the priority of which depends on the individual features and preferences of both the candidate and the organization. Employees are a representation of your brand every day through every e-mail, phone call, and communication. With each of these touch points, you have the potential to leave the client feeling positive, negative, or neutral, so best to tip the odds in your organization's favor by ensuring your employees are a good fit for your organization.

> **Employees are a representation of your brand every day through every e-mail, phone call, and communication. With each of these touch points, you have the potential to leave the client feeling positive, negative, or neutral.**

The third category of fit is *fit for the manager* or, depending on the organization, the organization's leader. Remember, many times people leave managers, not companies. How often have you heard someone say, "I like my job, but I can't stand my manager"?

A person in that situation can always try to find a different role in the organization because he or she likes the organization. If that employee finds a manager who is a better fit, chances are that employee will be much better positioned to achieve engagement for your organization.

Also, if one employee leaves a manager, that's one thing: some people just don't fit each other. But if you have many employees leaving a particular manager, you may have a problem with the manager being a fit. Many employees are seeking to find a manager who covers their back and is someone they can trust; from there, employees may seek a manager that builds workplace relationships that help them get their job done better.

Then the fourth category of fit is a *fit for the team*. You want to make sure that employees have a good team around them to build relationships with, colleagues that they can trust; and someone to cover their back. You need to know that they can all get the work done together and build a collaborative workplace. If you don't anticipate a new hire will work well with the existing team, you've got a problem, and if an existing team doesn't get along, you may have key insight into the cause behind departmental problems. Most of us can think of a time when we removed a drama-causing member from the team and how it changed the dynamics in a positive way for everyone.

I'm really surprised by how many people don't ask to meet the coworkers that they would be working with daily when they're interviewing for a particular job. For that matter, it's surprising that employers don't bring in candidates to meet the team more often! Does that failure represent a time issue, or is it that everyone is afraid that they won't like the other party? Can you imagine how rewarding that would be to employees to be asked to be a part of the hiring process? Even if such a meeting wasn't in a formal interview, you could walk the candidate around and have employees (and potential future coworkers) take a few minutes to share with the job candidate what they are working on; that, too, would serve as ego-boosting recognition for some employees.

Take note, though: know which employees would be excited about such a showcase and which ones would totally hate being interrupted or put on the spot without notice. You're looking for a win–win situation, not to start a relationship off on the wrong foot! When you think about it, you spend so much time at work, especially when you're in an environment where you rub shoulders with the same team members all of the time, that having a good fit with your team can take on an outsized importance.

It's amazing how many employers just want to get the job filled with someone "good," without really thinking about the concept of fit. Isn't that what we all would like—to find someone good? By paying attention to the fit piece, we can ensure that we do find someone that is good, intentionally. I was recently consulting with a client hiring a new controller and as we looked at the top candidate, I asked my client, the leader, how he would need to work with the candidate and he commented, "Oh, I didn't even think of that." Once we had the discussion of how the leader could use his talents to set the controller up for success—as he, himself, had the skills needed for the role—the leader got even more excited about the candidate. He felt that he and the candidate had a good fit that would allow them to work well together. Unintentionally, there is sometimes a hyper focus on the role without really understanding this concept of fit.

Similarly, it's amazing how many candidates just focus on getting the job versus thinking about the four components of fit and how they might affect their experience at work. And yet if the workplace is right, if the manager is right, if the role is right, and if you've got a great team surrounding you, how engaged is a person going to be? Very engaged. Once all parties have reached an agreement about the offer, if a person is going to be disengaged in the workplace, the culprit causing the problem can usually be found in the form of a lack of fit in one or more of these categories.

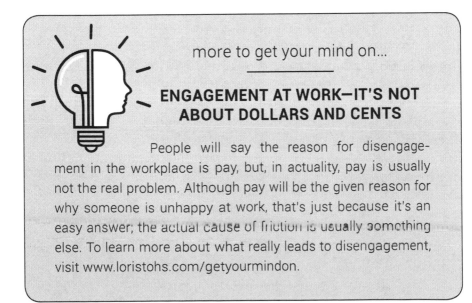

more to get your mind on...

ENGAGEMENT AT WORK—IT'S NOT ABOUT DOLLARS AND CENTS

People will say the reason for disengagement in the workplace is pay, but, in actuality, pay is usually not the real problem. Although pay will be the given reason for why someone is unhappy at work, that's just because it's an easy answer; the actual cause of friction is usually something else. To learn more about what really leads to disengagement, visit www.loristohs.com/getyourmindon.

A candidate may look good on paper—that résumé might be the best one you've seen in years—but if the potential employee does not have the right talent for the role or the organization, or if the candidate does not get along well with the manager or the other team members, it's time to look past the paper and trust your gut.

Your job is to align your employee and your organization for success. If the candidate simply does not fit the role, the organization, the manager, or the team, despite all the promise you see on that résumé, you're not doing either one of you any favors by hiring the candidate. The result will likely be the candidate doing uninspired, résumé-dampening work for a period of time before quietly stepping out the door or, even worse, leaving the organization in a tsunami of drama that makes *Game of Thrones* look like an HR training video.

Ask yourself whether you want Mr. Right versus Mr. Right Now. You'll know the right fit when you find it, and trust me when I say it's worth waiting for. Mr. Right Now may seem great at the moment, but in a few months, you may be kicking yourself when you are having to sit down to "have the conversation" around his performance.

HOW THE WHOLE PERSON MODEL WORKS WITH THE HUMAN CAPITALIZATION MODEL

I've introduced two models so far: the Human Capital Optimization Model and the Whole Person Model. That's all well and good, you might say, but how do these two models relate to each other? Remember, the Human Capital Optimization Model is a concept, the framework to get an understanding of how the business strategy and the human capital strategy align. This is designed with the goal of getting the best and the most out of your people and leaving them engaged and happier and healthier for it, both inside and outside of the organization. The Whole Person Model is a hands-on mechanism that drills down into the person and ties to putting the Human Capital Optimization Model into action.

If you look at the Human Capital Optimization Model (see chapter 2), in the middle, I've put the core organizational business components of culture, leadership, strategy, and brand. To the left side, I've placed the selection of new talent or new employees who you are bringing in to build the organization, and on the right side, I have existing employees who are in the organization today. Sometimes I refer to those on the left as the army that you want to bring in versus the army that exists today, those on the right. This is not to say that those already serving ultimately have to be dismissed. While the army you have may not currently be operating in the exact way you want it to yet, it is possible that with some adjustments—training, equipment, the rewriting or reassigning of job roles—you can bring your current army into closer alignment with your ideal force.

The Whole Person Model explains how you select the people—the new employees on the left or the existing employees on the right in the Human Capital Optimization Model—who match up with and carry out the core functions of upholding the culture, leadership, strategy, and brand of your organization. All of these components need to be considered and aligned to each other. Too often the people strategy is aligned only in numbers to the business strategy rather than in terms of the type, the feel, the engagement, and the like.

In addition, the organizational goals will not be achieved if your potential and existing employees don't fit with their job roles, the organization, the manager, and the team, because when fit is lacking, employees won't be engaged and jobs will not be done in the optimal way with consistency. Unfortunately, there is usually a time lag in recognizing this disengagement, so sometimes you may abandon a business idea or department while wondering what the root of the failure may be, and you haven't dug deep enough to know if it's the product, the delivery, the operations, or the people running these components. This fit depends on the strengths—the talent, skills, knowledge, and experience—of the person, and these strengths are the focus of the Whole Person Model.

CONCLUSION: A WHOLE PERSON APPROACH

Next time you find yourself scratching your head, wondering why a promising job candidate turned flat upon arrival in the role or an existing performer who has received hours of training and been on the job for years still can't seem to perform up to standard, you'll have the Whole Person Model to dispel any confusion and bring into sight where the issue lies. Skills, knowledge, values, and experience all play a role, as can fit with the team, manager, and organization, yet often it's a case of a disconnect between a person's talent and the job role. No amount of training or experience can overcome the error of putting someone with Talents A, B, and C with a job that requires Talents X, Y, and Z.

Part II of this book will provide practical guidance on how to use the Whole Person Model to attract and select the right people for the job and then get the best performance out of them, in all levels and roles of the organization. This model provides a whole person/whole organization approach to foster alignment between the employee and the job role. Add to that the larger Human Capital Optimization Model, and you have the tools you need to align your people strategy with your business identity to enable your people—your most valuable asset—to achieve the higher performance and productivity you seek.

PART II

get your mind on...
HIRING

How much time would you take to sign a million-dollar contract?

GETTING THE MOST FROM THE MILLION-DOLLAR CONTRACT

Creating Talent-Based Job Profiles

You've heard me say this before and I'll continue to emphasize my point: people are your most valuable asset. This is not just in terms of the value they add to your organization but also in terms of how much they cost your organization. Think about it this way: If you hire someone at an annual salary of $100,000 and he or she stays with your organization for ten years, you will have invested, at a minimum, $1 million in that employee, not accounting for pay raises, health care costs, retirement account matching, continuing education, and other benefits. One million dollars! That's a big investment. Numbers may vary, but the point remains the same. Over a ten-year period, you will have invested a lot in a single employee. Add that up across employees and your investment is huge. Let's look at it another way. Depending upon the size of your organization, how much time would you take to sign a million-dollar contract? I would guess that you would take much more time than you currently take to select the right person for the right role.

It's true, some employees won't make it to ten years' seniority, but then that's not an improvement on the situation, as the cost to your organization will be higher in that case. You will have to hire a replacement for the lost employee, laying out thousands more dollars in recruiting, hiring, and training the replacement, in addition to losing money due to reduced organizational productivity while the vacancy is being filled. In 2012, when the Center for American Progress reviewed thirty case studies on the actual monetary cost of employee turnover, they found that the median cost of job turnover was around 20 percent of the annual salary for the position. This number stayed fairly consistent across pay ranges, although the cost climbed disproportionately when the job required highly specialized skills or was highly compensated.[1]

> **When you have leaders who are making buying decisions and signing contracts, troublesome hiring decisions may cost you even more.**

In some instances when you have leaders who are making buying decisions and signing contracts, troublesome hiring decisions may cost you even more. In one organization we consulted with, it was discovered after their CIO was terminated that he had signed long-term contracts that were not good decisions, yet the organization was obligated to honor them. These contracts ended up costing the company millions of dollars. So not only did the company take financial hits on the dissolution of the CIO's contract and the cost of finding his replacement, but they also had to deal with the fact that the decisions he had made while there cost the company a lot of money, even long after he was gone.

Most of my clients want to get the most out of their investment in their employees, which is why we spend so much of our time together working on getting their selection and hiring process right. That process is the focus of this part of the book, and it will help you attain the same benefits as my clients by putting into action the left side of the Human Capital Optimization Model (see chapter 2, Figure 2.1). This is the side of the model that focuses on bringing high-performing employees on board. Every time you approve or sign an employment agreement, I want you to start thinking of it as a million-dollar contract so you can give hiring and selection the attention it really deserves.

WHAT JOB ARE WE FILLING ANYWAY? THE NUMBER ONE STEP MOST COMPANIES OVERLOOK

It's time to hire. But who's the right person for the role? Speaking of a million dollars, that's the million-dollar question. If you could answer it right the majority of the time, imagine the positive impact it would have on your organization. Envision what your teams and departments would look like if you had the best and the brightest filling each role and if the roles were the right ones aligned to each team member's talents—talented salespeople selling, smart programmers programming, creative designers innovating, and influential managers managing, all of them effectively. Talk about a well-oiled machine!

Some skeptics may argue that this is a great vision but a hard one to achieve. Others may say, "we have that already." But do they? Do these organizations have their people performing at a consistent level consistently? How much of the time really do organizations have their people performing at a high level? World-class results do not come from part-time talent.

ABOUT THAT PART-TIME TALENT . . .

When I say, "Part-time talent doesn't make world-class performance," it makes people pause. The innate truth in this statement resonates. Yet, I want to be clear that when I say this, I'm not referring to part time in terms of the amount of work put in—I have nothing against twenty-hour-a-week jobs, I assure you! What matters to me (and should matter to all managers) is that the person in a job role has all the talent it takes to do the job well. If I have only 50 percent of the talent aligned to the job responsibilities, then we're losing. No matter how much time put in by the employee, the job will not be done as well as it could be. You need over 75 percent of the talent alignment to achieve world-class performance on that job. Most people in their jobs, even though we're paying them for full-time hours, are essentially working part time because they don't have the talent to maximize the job role. The body's in the seat, but only twenty hours of the forty-hour week are being put in to the degree that the organization needs. In the real world, you know the perfect match of job and talent when you see it—you will catch glimpses of greatness in job performance, and you'll be wishing you could have four more employees just like that one.

Here's a hint for you too: if you get the right person with the right talent in the right role and find yourself with a world-class performer on your hands: recognize that talent and work with it. World-class performers won't stay unless you provide that talent with positive reinforcement, additional challenges that let them take their talent to the next level, and peers and other coworkers who strive just as hard as they do. If your world-class performer feels like no one else in your organization is at their level, he or she is going to leave to find a workplace that does have that kind of talent at work. I know—I've done this! Boredom is a motivation killer; and the last thing you want to do is undermine world-class performance, because achieving world-class performance is the difference that will make the difference.

Getting the right employees is completely within your reach, if you are using the right process. The overall structure of the process I recommend is likely going to sound familiar to you, as it builds on the norms used in business today; what I am going to do is add to and fine-tune what you already know with what you don't yet know or maybe aren't yet doing, to have a huge impact. Here's how the high-level selection process typically goes at most companies.

1. Recruit

2. Interview

3. Make offer and hire

One very important step is missing from this standard process. The process should actually look like this:

1. Create a talent-based role profile

2. Recruit

3. Interview (which I refer to as *selection*)

4. Make offer and hire (which I refer to as *hiring*)

Most companies skip step 1 altogether or do a poor job with it. Instead of writing what I call a talent-based *role profile*, organizations may pull an old job description and use it for the recruiting process, which saves time in the short run but often creates pain down the line when the wrong candidates keep applying—or the candidate who seems right for the job gets hired and then flops.

Those companies that do write up a new job description often pull it together too quickly and without enough input from the department manager or the manager who will be managing the new hire. Alternately, the problem may be that they use the existing job description without thinking about what may have changed in the business that affects the role, or they may fail to consider the component of talent when creating the job description. Either way, the job description usually focuses on job skills, knowledge, experience, and the standard legal HR jargon. These are all important elements to use when weighing the appropriateness of a job candidate for the position you're hiring for, but as we now know from the Whole Person Model (see chapter 3), talent is at the core of any successful employee hire and the key differentiator in world-class performance.

A role profile is more detailed than a job description: it defines the role by the outcomes the role is designed to achieve and categorizes those outcomes in key areas of work. Those key areas are evaluated and defined by key behaviors and talents that align with the work. A good role profile also identifies the percentage of time each aspect of the work is performed. The necessary skills, knowledge, and experience to successfully perform the job role are defined clearly, but talent is the biggest component.

Let's go back to the percentage of time component. Common sense would tell you that the greater the percentage of time a person is expected to spend concentrating on a particular aspect of a job role, the stronger the job candidate's talents should be in that area. However, I find many times we are squeezing into the role the person we like best on a personal level and failing to look at the talent components. Many times there are 15-20 bullets

> **The greater the percentage of time a person is expected to spend concentrating on a particular aspect of a job role, the stronger the job candidate's talents should be in that area.**

listed for key responsibilities and they are all across the board. You might be asking yourself now, "Do we do this?" Regardless of your answer, keep in mind that this approach is never intentional: we simply fall into the trap of really liking a candidate for a certain part of him or her and not looking at the whole person. And then what happens? Unfortunately, those things we didn't notice in the beginning are the things that drive us crazy six months later.

For instance, I once was hiring an executive director for a non-profit organization. As I worked with the board members to facilitate the process, we thoroughly evaluated the key job areas and the behaviors we were looking for to achieve the desired outcomes from the executive director. In particular, we determined the role was 60 percent fund-raising and public awareness, 20 percent programming, 10 percent operations and financial, and 10 percent management. After clearly defining the role in this way, we built a role profile in accordance with this definition.

When it came time to review the candidates, we discovered that Deanna, the candidate everyone loved, did not have the talent for the fund-raising component, which was defined as 60 percent of the role. I completely agreed that she had great talent at programming, was a master at implementing operations, and was a delightful person, but the role profile we were hiring for was for a nonprofit that needed to be reinvigorated from a brand and funding perspective, and that was a huge gap for Deanna. Without the key talents to raise funds, influence others, and build the brand and relationships, the nonprofit would not be able to financially support the programs to implement. Given the time and attention we had spent on defining the role profile accurately, the *aha*'s came very easily to the team. In addition to realizing that Deanna was not, in fact, the right person for the role, they also recognized that a big reason for the pattern of high turnover in this role previously was due to them not hiring someone with the talent for fund-raising.

Here's the truth. If you ignore talent and only focus on the more commonly considered skills, knowledge, and experience, you are going to hire employees who underperform. You may get lucky with a high performer some of the time, but why leave a million-dollar hire to chance? From now on, before you jump into that next hire or replacement, step back and ask the question, "What talents are essential to the success of this role and in what amount?"

By clarifying and confirming what you are looking for and including all relevant parties in the decision-making process before writing up a role profile with talent at the core, you can attract more of the right candidates and recognize them when they walk through your door. Now, let's look at the first of the four steps in the selection process in detail, tweaked to hire right for the million-dollar contract (the remaining chapters in part II of the book cover the other three steps—recruit, select, and hire.)

GOT TALENT? DESIGNING THE PERFECT ROLE PROFILE

Most companies know the importance of hiring right for the C-suite, but many don't spend nearly enough time hiring for roles below the top tier of the organization. Yes, executives are essential, but that doesn't negate the value of the rest of the players. What's more, unconscious justifications for moving as quickly through the hiring process as possible abound. People want to focus on doing their jobs, not writing up role profiles or job descriptions and looking at résumés. Oh, but that *is* part of their job!

Selecting new employees is time consuming and takes attention away from other projects. Sometimes the justification for rushing through the hiring process is more overt, like when HR has a time-to-hire metric that it's trying to keep low. And we can pretend as much as we like that the proper people are included in this selection process, but we may not have all the individuals we need involved in the selection process. Those who will be managing and collaborating with the new employee on a day-to-day basis and your HR partners should all have key involvement in the selection of the right candidates for the job, even if including more people in the process slows down the show.

Creating a whole person, talent-based role profile begins with getting the interested parties in the same room—hiring manager, HR, and ideally the department head—to discuss the needs of the job. This is the first place where the selection process typically goes astray, with HR having one set of job duties and preferred qualifications in mind and the hiring manager having a different idea of what kind of person is needed and the role of the new hire. With everyone in the room, the different parties who have a stake in the new employee's success can each contribute to the conversation and ultimately align expectations. This lays the groundwork for the creation of effective job profiles that lead to successful recruiting and hiring down the line.

more to get your mind on...

A SAMPLE ROLE PROFILE

To view a sample role profile, go to www.loristohs.com/getyourmindon.

As you dig into creating the role profile, this first thing I recommend is to white board what success looks like in this role. Who are your best people and what behaviors do they portray? Describe them. What does this person look like, figuratively speaking? When I do this exercise with my clients, interestingly enough, when we go back to the list we have created together, on average 90 percent of the items will be—guess what?—*talent* based.

As mentioned in the previous chapter, many companies are not looking at talent when they hire, and yet, when they take the time to define what a successful candidate should look like, talent is at the core! The talent gap is a big one and the one that makes the difference. So what about skills, knowledge, and experience? Yes, those also show up on the list during brainstorms, and we may use those as screening criteria as well. Of course, we wouldn't hire a physician or an architect who lacked the proper education and certifications, but we need to identify candidates who also have the talents that play well with this education or it's not very helpful to the job role or the organization.

Remember that skills can always be taught, knowledge can continually be acquired, and experience can always be gained; in contrast, talents are innate. They can't be taught; they can't even really be coached...unless you are only looking for mediocrity. (For those of you who have tried, you know any effects are often temporary and the entire process is frustrating.)

Either a person is a strong empath or he's not. Either a person has the natural talent to invent or she doesn't. You can't teach touch. Set yourself up for success by designing a role profile that will identify candidates who possess the right talents. Need someone who can defuse conflict between two parties? Your role profile better specify someone with the talent to mediate. Need someone to find new uses for an old product? Make sure the role profile calls for someone with a talent to ideate. Do you wonder why some people pick something up so much faster than other? Ahhh, that's talent! *Talent can't be taught!*

> **Skills can always be taught, knowledge can continually be acquired, and experience can always be gained; in contrast, talents are innate.**

Notice again that I am using the term *role profile*, not *job description*. Every organization uses job descriptions for recruiting, but a role profile is what I ask my clients to create before writing up the job description. It is built based on the Whole Person Model. A role profile helps us to clearly define the key categories of work and responsibilities of the role and allows us to price the role as well. A role profile should include everything—every detail, every responsibility, every interaction, every expectation—about the job that you can think of and the talents, skills, knowledge, and experience of the ideal person to be doing it, which is probably more information that you can cram into your average job description or want ad! The emphasis in the role profile, though, is always on identifying the talents of the ideal person to fill the job.

Once created, the role profile can be used to do two things: (a) create a job description and (b) write an ad that will be used to recruit candidates online, in the newspaper, via recruiters, and so on. When the job description is written, the essential elements of the role profile are identified and added to the information that HR and the legal department must include to be in compliance with the rules and regulations they have to follow when advertising a job. The job description is the front-facing portion of the role profile, the announcement of what needs to be done and the kind of person needed to do it.

The ad is usually a portion of the job description, written in a sales-oriented way to attract candidates. I recommend leading a job ad with questions that get at talents: "Are you analytical? Can you see all the pieces of a problem and know what it takes to solve it? Do you stay calm in a crisis?" Ask and ye shall receive! When you move to writing up the job description and job ad, the recruiting process has begun.

get your hands on...

WRITING A TALENT-BASED ROLE PROFILE

Effective employee selection begins with an effective role profile, one that captures what it is you really want in a candidate. Instead of leaving that profile to chance, you can use the following process to cultivate success.

Get the team together: Start by gathering your team to brainstorm on what elements should go into the role profile. Be sure to involve all of the interested parties—HR, hiring manager, department head, and other stakeholders. Remember, the role profile is at the core of selection success, so all of the important and relevant people should be part of this process early on.

Define the job: With the key players gathered, you can begin to define the role you are trying to fill. What does the role entail? What are its key responsibilities, tasks, and expectations? Here's where you describe and quantify (using percentages) in detail how the employee will be spending her time in the role, whether preparing annual budgets, running training seminars, or traveling to client sites. Instead of drawing up a long list of bullet points, I recommend that you categorize the key work areas into a handful of buckets and then put the details within those categories.

Describe the candidate: With a clear sense of what the role entails, you are ready to describe the ideal person to fill the role. Brainstorm on what skills, knowledge, experience, values, and—most important—talents the ideal candidate will possess.

To get at talents, ask the team to take turns describing the person you're looking for in a behavioral way, for example, someone who gets projects done on time or can correct employees without upsetting them. Here's another way to frame the question: If you could have five more of a person from your organization for the role, who would it be? Describe the outstanding talents of that person, such as "great at communicating technical information in a simple way," or "has a capability for linear thinking and is process oriented."

As you and your team figure out the talents, skills, knowledge, experiences, and values an individual needs to be successful in the role you're defining, you will generate everything needed to write up an effective role profile, which will serve as the springboard for the job description and job ad. With an accurate and talent-based role profile in hand, you'll have a foundational tool for finding what (and who) you need.

CONCLUSION: OPENING YOUR MIND TO ALL OF THE POSSIBILITIES

Sometimes my role during a brainstorm to create the role profile is to break some of the traditional ways of thinking. For example, I remind clients not to assume the person needs a particular kind of degree or even a college degree. Ask yourself, if the candidate had all of the talents the job required, would it matter whether they had a certain degree? (Admittedly, some roles need certain levels of education.) Don't make assumptions about required skills or experience, either. If the person had the right talents, would you be willing to take the time to train him or her and get the candidate up to speed on the industry or the position? At this point, working to make a list of must-haves versus nice-to-haves is a good idea. Although we hope to find the candidate with all the characteristics we've identified, sometimes we will need to identify those items of most importance to us. Talent can't be taught; skills, knowledge, and experience can be acquired! So always keep talents at the forefront of what you are looking for in a candidate.

WIDENING THE FUNNEL

Recruiting and Interviewing to Make the Right Hire

I f you have done a good job of creating a talent-based role profile, you will have laid the groundwork for recruiting the right candidates. You are ready to turn the role profile into a job description and a recruiting ad so the recruiting can begin. One thing to note about recruiting is that we often look in the expected place rather than the most productive place for job candidates. Let me give you an example. I was working with an advertising firm that was seeking a project manager. If we had used the standard recruiting approach that many companies use, we would have focused on looking for someone with experience in agency work—someone who had the skills, knowledge, and experience of being in this field.

Now, the advertising environment is very creative, open, and full of big ideas, while project management involves a lot of process and structure. So, if you are trying to hire an advertising project manager and you're looking for someone from the advertising industry and nowhere else, you might be missing out on a lot of good candidates with a talent for process and flow who are working in other industries. Sometimes those best practices from other environments can lend great value when they migrate to different fields. Most people who like process and flow may not be in advertising; they're typically in more structured work environments.

Yes, of course, the ultimate package would be someone who has the talent of the project manager with experience in advertising. But if you're looking for a project manager, what's more important: that the person has the talent to be a great project manager or that the person has the experience of working in advertising? Here's a hint: you can provide the experience of working in advertising, but you're not going to build the talent of being an effective project manager if the recruit doesn't bring that talent to your shop with him or her. Within months, you will be frustrated that your project workflow is not smooth and efficient.

What ended up happening in this particular case is that we kept our funnel wide and hired someone with project management experience in the financial industry. True, finance is not advertising, but the talent for project management was there, and that's what we were looking for. This new hire, in applying her talent to a new work environment, was able to share some of the best practices from her industry. When she introduced new efficiencies to the ad agency's processes, the result was increased engagement across the office. Talk about a win-win!

more to get your mind on...

A SAMPLE JOB ADVERTISEMENT

When it becomes time to create the job ad, it's time to pull out your role profile and make sure that your ad writer translates the desired talents—which you and your team have painstakingly compiled—into attention-grabbing lead-off questions. *Can you identify all the facets of a problem and know how to solve it? Do you see the details that others miss? Are you the person others turn to, to bring two opposing sides to an agreement?* A great job ad is not unlike a great singles ad: it should quickly attract the kind of person you're looking for! The job ad should describe what responsibilities the job entails, and it should list the skills, knowledge, and experience a candidate needs. Talents are the essential part of a great job ad, but don't simply list the talents needed. Go into detail about what you're looking for. Remember, talents are what will make your ideal candidate an engaged and productive employee. Let your job ad, a shorter version of your role profile, help you reel in your ideal person for your next million-dollar contract. To see a sample job advertisement, go to www.loristohs.com/getyourmindon.

RECRUITING: SOURCING THE BEST CANDIDATES

When you're ready to recruit, take time to answer the question of where best to source your candidates. Instead of going the typical matching-the-industry route—"I need somebody in advertising" or "I need someone in banking"—widen your funnel and try to attract candidates outside the industry who may have the talent that you seek. You can always teach skills and knowledge and provide experience, but if the talent is missing at the start, it will always be missing, setting the employee up to underperform and to have lackluster performance.

Industry finds would be great, but they are not your only option. Does having the knowledge and the experience in a given industry help? It does, because a person will already speak the language. Yet, if that person doesn't have the talent, the person and the role will never be a good fit and you will have inconsistent performance. When you recruit, I want you to think about widening your funnel rather than narrowing it. Be open to lots of different ways of finding good candidates. How can you grab all the candidates that you can to align to the talents you are looking for?

GO BEYOND THE SHINY INTERVIEW AND SCREEN FOR TALENT

Making the Cut: The Initial Screening

Your funnel is filled; now it's time to screen the sea of possible candidates to decide which ones are worth your time (and theirs!) to bring in for an interview. For the most part, this is a straightforward process, which you likely already have in place at your organization. You may take the candidate through an online screening process, where they complete an application over the Internet, or you may go through résumés directly yourself. How you design the selection process will depend in part on the job's classification (exempt vs. nonexempt) and the number of positions you are trying to fill (low volume vs. high volume). It will also depend on how much you are willing and able to invest in the process.

If you're not hiring very many people that often or if you have a small organization, it may not be worth your time and expense to create a customized online screening assessment. If you're a larger organization or a smaller one on the rise, you might find that the investment in an online assessment allows you to save both time and money in the long run when candidates who will not be a good fit for your organization are eliminated from the search early in the process. Many times I find that companies are investing a lot of human-capital hours of time in manual processes when they can insert an online or technology solution for efficiency.

Regardless of the form of the initial screening—online or through a manual résumé review—most organizations call and screen the candidates before setting up interviews to get a feel for who they want to bring in. Although the phone screening is far from your final determining factor, you can gain quite a bit of insight from a fifteen-minute conversation and save everyone time in the long run when the fit isn't right. Make sure you not only screen for core requirements of the role but start to integrate the talent assessment questions. Once phone screenings are complete, you are ready to trim down your list, eliminating those who didn't do well and inviting in those who show promise.

Tell Me More: The Interview

Next comes the familiar face-to-face interview phase. This process will, of course, vary organization by organization, but generally it involves a series of in-person interviews of the smaller group of candidates you choose to call in. On the one hand, the interview phase is a standard process with which every organization is familiar. On the other hand, I don't want you to take anything about the interview process for granted. Remember, metaphorically or literally speaking, you need to look at this hire as a decision about a long-term investment—remember that million-dollar contract. Put in the time now to create a high-quality interview experience to ensure that you have useful data to crunch when making your final selections. Here are some important considerations to keep in mind when conducting the interview:

- Be sure to give candidates time to interact with others in the office to see how they get along with people—a combination of quick interactions and opportunities to really engage. Some people are personable at a moment's notice and some need a little time to warm up. Neither approach is inherently good or bad, but it's important information to know depending on the role you are hiring for. Is the candidate a fit not just for the role but for the team and for the organization?

- When you are conducting the interviews, whatever question process you use—behavioral interviewing, et cetera—make sure you are aware of what you are listening for. Many answers might seem good, but are they linking back to what you are looking for in the role profile?

- Ask everyone who interacts with this person for feedback. For example, my organization strategically has the assistant who greets the candidate and walks him through the building evaluate the candidate later. Is he kind to all people? Is he nervous? How was the candidate's demeanor with the customers he passed? Is the candidate engaging? No judgment is required, just a feel. We have had a few instances when high-level candidates who have come through treated the staff poorly. That behavior immediately signaled that the candidates clearly were not a fit for us, as our organizational culture values treating all employees with respect, no matter what their level in the organization's hierarchy (see "More to Get Your Mind On: Getting the Group's Feedback" later in the chapter for information on a survey to gather everyone's input on a job candidate).

- If your organization has the resources, design and use a customized selection tool to scientifically score each candidate during the interview process and assess their fit for the role (see the next section, "Testing the Waters: Talent

Assessment," for more details). Such tools are usually administered online, consist of questions of differing importance whose answers are averaged into a weighted final score, and ensure early in the process that the candidate meets mandatory job requirements.[1] Other types of assessment can also be administered, such as personality tests, talent assessments, behavioral simulations, and ability tests.

- For leadership roles, take your time. This is dating before marriage. Meet in many different environment types and settings. You need to see how the candidate interacts in many circumstances. Also take time to meet spouses and life partners to gain insight into their comfort level with supporting the candidate's commitment to the job, especially with a relocation. An unhappy partner can lead to poor performance and retention. Helping the partner to have a clear understanding of the role, the environment, and the internal support team is important. It also gives you a sense of what's important to the partner as a family member in the candidate's life. Without a holistic alignment of the executive job candidate's life and the requirements of the job role, a good fit will be hard, if not impossible, to achieve.

When it comes to interviews, l am also going to say out loud what most people won't admit and others don't realize. It's very challenging to identify through just an interview process how

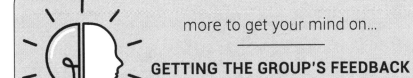

more to get your mind on...

GETTING THE GROUP'S FEEDBACK

I recommend creating a quick, online feedback survey for anyone who has been part of the interview process to answer a few questions about the job candidate, her qualifications, and her fit. Use a rating scale for quantitative scores and comments for qualitative detail. Then conduct a group conversation about the candidate. I find sometimes that feedback details get missed or opinions get swayed into one direction or another if a person of influence is in the room. Visit www.loristohs.com/getyourmindon for a sample survey your organization can use to gather feedback from the team.

well a person will fill a job role. Yes, we go through the interview process; yes, we ask good questions; and yes, we listen carefully. Even so, here's the reality. When we hire someone on the basis of an interview, we are mostly guessing that they'll be able to do the job! Frightening but true.

In a recent speaking engagement with a group of HR leaders, we discussed this fact. Do you really feel comfortable that the talent you are hiring is right for both the organization and the individual? Do you have the right process in place? Do you take the time you need to make the right selection? Over 60 percent of the individuals at this engagement agreed that the existing process wasn't the best. More than one person was able to recall a time when someone was hired simply because HR was up against a days-to-fill metric and a job candidate seemed good enough for the role. This is not the basis on which someone should be brought into your organization! Poor hiring decisions lead to turnover, which leads to the need for more hiring to be done. That's a self-defeating cycle. We need to pay attention to filling the role profile, not just hitting a deadline. Don't rush the process to fill the role. Success is when someone stays and is a good fit, so take the time to achieve true success.

Those of us doing the hiring have to ask ourselves, are we as certain as we can be that we are not just filling a spot and choosing the best of the worst candidates? Are we jumping to hire because we are desperate and have a role to fill and we need a pulse in a seat? You've heard me refer to this as *hiring Mr. Right vs. Mr. Right Now*. Many of us have hired Ms. Right Now, and what always happens? We find ourselves managing performance issues within their first months of employment.

Yes, we are the employer and we have the right to change our minds or dismiss someone, but a wrong hire costs the organization time and money, and these are people's lives we are dealing with. They have accepted the job, possibly turned down other offers, and maybe even relocated, all on good faith that your organization is clear that they are the right people for the position you're hiring for. Don't play with someone's life just because you didn't do your due diligence at the time of hiring and you're in the stronger position and have the legal right to so. Remember this is another element of being in tune with your human capital consciousness. In addition, think about how such behavior reflects on your culture and brand.

get your hands on...

TESTING THE WATERS USING A TALENT ASSESSMENT

One critical element that increases my confidence level greatly when selecting a candidate for a job role is using a talent assessment. We make sure that any candidate who is being seriously considered to fill a position has completed an assessment of his talents so we can see whether the candidate really has what it takes to perform well at the job role. Ultimately, it's talent, not title, that matters.

You may administer a talent assessment before bringing someone in for an interview, at the interview, or after the interview. This will depend upon the role, the number of candidates for the role you are hiring for, and the type of assessment you are using. The talent assessment is one of the essential elements of the Human Capital Optimization Model that will help you make sure that you hire employees with the right talent for the job.

There are many, many different types of assessments that you can use, such as skills assessments, experience assessments, personality assessments, behavioral interviews, role simulations, and talent assessments.[2] We focus mostly on the talent assessments. Many are available to use, but you have to find the right one for your organization, the particular roles you are hiring for, and the number of roles you are hiring for. The idea behind the use of any of these assessments is to get a sense of whether the person that you have in front of you has what it takes to do the job that you need filled under the circumstances and in the environment that person will encounter in your workplace. This is why a role profile is so helpful to have: it's a constant reminder that skills are only one part of the equation.

For example, perhaps you need someone with mechanical skills who can fix anything. You get a number of candidates who can MacGyver their way out of any situation. Your cup runneth over! However, a personality assessment or a behavioral simulation will give you a better idea of who is going to thrive in your shop's high-volume, high-stress, everything's-an-emergency, constant triage work environment. It's probably not going to be the person low on Openness to Experience and high on Neuroticism on a Big Five Personality Test (personality assessment) or the one who, when given a sample list of projects that just came into the shop that morning, hems and haws for twenty minutes and ultimately can't prioritize them (behavioral simulation).[3] A couple of key tips to think about when assessing a person's talent and fit are the following:

- If you are using an off-the-shelf tool that measures an individual's talent and personality, make sure it aligns to the role.
- If you are using a role-specific tool, make sure you couple it with a fit interview (e.g., two successful sales candidates from the same industry may not both fit well with your organizational culture) and/or a simulation immersion, which helps provide a hands-on and real-life view of the job.

An alternative approach to candidate assessment could incorporate a customized selection tool. This is something you build or commission to scientifically score your applicants on the behaviors that will show up consistently with the job, thus gauging their suitability for the position. Many companies can help you create a customized assessment. Some key steps included in this process are studying your top performers and low performers to figure out what it is that makes them so successful or unsuccessful at those jobs. If you don't already have people in those roles, then consult your talent-based role profile and figure out what your candidate needs to succeed. Once you've isolated the strengths that seem to contribute to job role success, come up with questions that reveal the talent, as well as a scoring system.

Keep in mind that your scoring system must be valid and stand up in a court of law; that is, it cannot discriminate between people on a basis other than job skills. For example, you may have all young, white men in your IT department right now, but that doesn't mean someone has to be young, white, or male to succeed in IT. The nice thing about a customized selection tool is that it can be laser-like in its focus on fit to the role. Some sway away from constructing such tools, as they can be quite labor intensive to create. However, depending on the importance of the role or the number of people needed in the same role, the effort can truly be worth the investment. The cost of building the assessment and administration oftentimes provides a great return versus hiring and rehiring and training and retraining talent.

There are pros and cons to each approach. An already existing general online selection tool is easier to use and costs less, whereas a customized selection instrument designed for the specific job you are hiring for is in-depth and more accurate but costs more because the organization has to develop it from scratch and for each role. General online personality assessments will provide you with information on a candidate's personality, which provides clues to whether there is fit with the role, team, and organization, while a selection tool assesses more specifically whether the behaviors needed for the job will show up consistently for this candidate. If your organization has the money and tolerance, it's most helpful to use a customized selection instrument when you are interviewing. However, for some organizations, the selection tool costs too much in both time and money, and a talent assessment tool can be a useful alternative. Having something that is measuring the level of talent and aligning that to the job role and the fit with the team is better than nothing at all.

MAKING YOUR SELECTION: SEEKING THE RIGHT FIT AND HIRING FOR THE LONG TERM

You've written a role profile that has talent at its core (see chapter 4); you've gotten creative about attracting candidates with the right talent, without getting narrowed into a single industry or skill set; you've interviewed the best candidates from the pool of choices; and you've assessed them for their strengths and/or talents. It's time to take the data generated from the interviews and talent-screening process and determine which of your final candidates has the right fit for the role, the manager, the team, and the organization. It's time to take out the Whole Person Model (see Figure 3.1 in chapter 3).

Selecting the Right Candidate Using the Whole Person Model

Let's say you have two good final candidates to fill a communications specialist role in the Customer Service Department of a large insurance company. Both candidates interviewed well, but they have different backgrounds and personalities. Which one do you choose? It's the moment of truth. Remember the must-haves and the like-to-haves lists you wrote up previously? (See the "Conclusion" of chapter 5.) Pull them out now. Oh, and don't forget you are at the point in the process where you are getting ready to commit to the proverbial million-dollar contract. No one wants to get this decision wrong: leaders, HR, or even the candidate herself. Take time now to see how each candidate holds up when you assess her against the Whole Person Model.

In addition to skills, knowledge, experience, and values, as you conduct your evaluation, keep talent at the forefront of your attention, too. If the candidate has the needed talent today, she will perform well in the new role and be a good long-term investment; if she lacks the talent, no amount of on-the-job training or mentoring will make up for it. Sometimes it is challenging to determine who is the best candidate, so step back and evaluate from the perspective of all components.

As you make your final selection on whom to offer the job, dig deep into fit, too (see Figure 3.2 in chapter 3). Ensure there will be fit with the job role, manager, team, and organizational culture. As you compare final candidates, think not just about who made a positive impression during the interview but also who showed the most potential to mesh well with the job and the organization. Think about the candidate's style as well as the manager's style: if the candidate needs a lot of ego stroking and the manager simply is not a hand holder, this pairing might not work. Consider the candidates' values, too, which will give insight into how well they

more to get your mind on...

IDENTIFYING IMPOSTORS WHO INTERVIEW WELL BUT TANK ON THE JOB

Many people ask me, "How can I know if a candidate is just a good interviewee"? Many of us have met people who were good in an interview; perhaps we've even seen them in action, charming the HR representative and hiring manager while wielding industry buzzwords like throwing stars. More than one person has talked their way into a great job by nailing the interview, but is the best interviewee always the best candidate for a job? How can an interviewer know if the job candidate who says all the right things can translate their talk into effective action in real life or instead just has the gift of gab? The key is to listen. Listen for patterns. Is the person able to give you depth consistently in an area? For someone to have talent in an area consistently, you have to hear it multiple times. If you are not hearing it in their examples, it's likely it's not going to show up consistently in the work performed. For more guidance, go to www.loristohs.com/getyourmindon.

will get along with the team and align with the beliefs in the organization. Last, allow those in the group who designed the original role profile to weigh in on the final selection, too.

It's been quite the process! When we consistently follow this process, we can clearly understand how we become the organization everyone wants to work for. The level of talent that exists in the organization is healthy, consistent, and engaged. People want to work for companies where the employees are happy and getting results! Here's a look at a sample process for a manager role, with the four essential steps and all the work in between.

Figure 5.1: Sample Sequence for Recruiting and Hiring

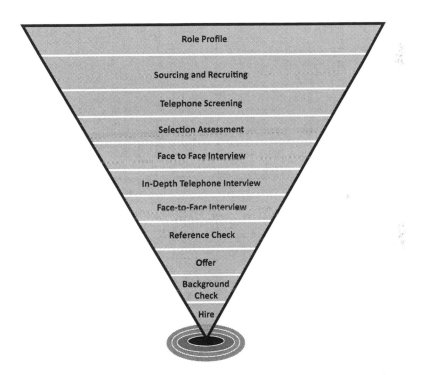

You've done a lot of work to find and select the right person for the job. Now it's time to get your mind on hiring right to set the stage for effective onboarding and the world-class performance your efforts deserve.

Negotiations: Getting Down to Brass Tacks

Once you've made your final selection and offered the job, negotiations with the candidate may begin. Some may accept the job offer out of hand, bypassing negotiations entirely, and others may need to take time to decide about whether your organization is the right fit for them, just as you took time to decide that they were the right fit for your organization. Consider an employee insightful enough to seriously consider whether your organization is right for them a good sign! That means you're all taking this hiring process seriously. A good employment situation can last longer than some marriages, so do not begrudge someone who is not willing to jump into the commitment without thinking through the match: you don't want this to be a case of get hired in haste, repent at leisure. Remember, in our job environment, if anyone is repenting

> **Don't let the routine nature of the process let you overlook this as an early opportunity to brand yourself with the new employee.**

about the hire that means the employee is disengaged, and you already know how destructive disengagement can be (see chapter 1). Also, expect top-performing sales talent to negotiate. That's what you are hiring them to do in their role for your organization, so they will likely use that talent when hammering out an employment agreement with you.

Once you have signed a contract with your top pick, hiring procedures begin. Although this is generally a straightforward process with forms and paperwork, don't let the routine nature of the process let you overlook this as an early opportunity to brand yourself with the new employee. This is as much about the new employee choosing to work with you as it is about you choosing to hire him, so I recommend starting early with making a good impression. Few things can turn a new employee off as much as a nonresponsive manager or an HR department with an unorganized process. I have heard many horror stories from candidates about the process.

One person I know started a part-time contract job at an organization loosely affiliated with a state university. Because of her work status, she didn't think she was eligible for pension benefits, and the organization's HR person didn't clarify the situation or follow up on the matter when the employee didn't fill out the pension paperwork, yet another form in a huge stack to be filled out on the first day.

Months went by, and the organization's HR person took a job in a different department. The university's HR person eventually started trying to contact the employee about the pension paperwork, but she consistently used the wrong e-mail address, so the employee still was unaware of her pension participation status.

When the university's HR person finally managed to contact the employee, it was days before a tax deadline, and if the employee did not get her notarized paperwork in immediately, her department would be slapped with a not insignificant fine. The employee scrambled, spending the better part of a day downloading and filling out paperwork, tracking down a notary on a Friday afternoon in her small town, and express mailing the paperwork in. And once she did all that? Not one person acknowledged the receipt of the paperwork. Thank goodness for online delivery confirmation, or she'd still be wondering if they'd received the envelope! What started as a miss on day one turned an employee benefit into stress that could have been avoided.

As you move through the hiring process, remember that there's an emotional side to this process for the candidate. They have to separate from their previous organization—coworkers, bosses, responsibilities, old health insurance, 401(k)s, and more. They may have to deal with a counteroffer from their current employer. How you handle the hiring process from a qualitative perspective is important to getting off to a good start with your new hire.

Go the extra mile. Let HR get in touch to give tips on what the new environment is going to be like and what to expect their first day or week on the job. And how about hand-writing a note welcoming them aboard? Keep in mind that the new employee is going through a transition stage as well and make sure your organization stays connected to the employee in a way that works for your brand and her situation. This is human capital consciousness.

Note, too, that by creating a hiring experience consistent with your brand, you begin the process of educating the employee about the organizational culture. This lays the foundation for the new employee to adapt to the culture and learn how to emulate organizational values over time. As she becomes exposed to your brand, your employee can absorb it and carry on the brand image in the new role.

I recently hired a woman who had been with her previous company for seventeen years. She knew it was time to go, wanted something different, and had a good fit with the new organization, but nonetheless she was going through the difficult emotional aspects of leaving her coworkers and a company that had been good to her for many years. As we moved through her hiring process, I made sure to stay

> **By creating a hiring experience consistent with your brand, you begin the process of educating the employee about the organizational culture.**

connected with her in a personal and supportive way. The day before she turned in her letter of resignation to her old company, I called her. I acknowledged her emotion and complimented her on her loyalty. By showing her that we already valued her as a person and employee, I was not only expressing my genuine concern but also taking the opportunity to model the kind of attention and sensitivity that our organization's culture and brand emphasize and show that we truly cared about her as a person.

Although you will put far less time into communicating with those candidates who did not get the job, I encourage you to be respectful and personable when you let them know they are not receiving an offer for the position. I am amazed when, after going through multiple interviews, some do not get a call or, at minimum, an e-mail about the final decision. For me, this is again about respect for the person as a human being and an important brand builder or brand diminisher. Remember human capital consciousness. We need to be conscious of how we treat people that we interact with, in any manner, employees or not. Although these individuals are not the chosen candidate for this particular job, if they are people you want to keep in your talent bank, you may want to invite them to come back and interview when another job opens. They may also be a source of referrals for future positions—your network can never be too large when you're looking for good people to work for your organization!

This will come up again in chapter 8 on performance management, but believe me when I say that feedback is a gift. Don't be afraid to give it. Personally, I take the time to share with the candidates who do not get the job why they were not a fit for the role, give them feedback on how they did during the selection process, and even possibly advise them on the job role that would be the best fit for them. For example, with the startup company we opened, there were some who just were not a fit for constant change and volatility that would likely occur in a startup environment. I was very clear with them that we would be going through evolving change for likely the first two years, so that after the startup phase, we could potentially reengage. This is another opportunity to brand your organization well for the public.

Remember, when you're following the tenets of the Human Capital Optimization Model, as discussed in chapter 2, every interaction your organization and its representatives has with people within and outside of the organization is an opportunity to demonstrate the organization's culture, leadership, strategy, and brand. If yours is the kind of organization that says it places a high priority on clear communication and treating every person as an individual, you can't ignore those cultural values because you're interacting with someone who is not coming onboard at this moment. Building the brand of the HR or people team is important. How have you treated people through the process? My goal in running our organization was to leave candidates in a better place than when we met them. Whether we hired them or not, giving them new insights or feedback about themselves or something as simple as communicating often built the brand of HR.

CONCLUSION: ACKNOWLEDGING THE VALUE OF TALENT

You have just gained valuable insight for your organization into the time, effort, and resources needed to secure a talented employee who is primed to be a world-class performer. Those efforts are likely to pay off for years to come when you pair your employee with the proper training and support (see chapter 6), a great manager (see chapter 7), and effective performance management feedback (see chapter 8). You have made a million-dollar contract that is poised to pay off with a great return.

As you evaluate your selection processes in the future, keep in mind that current employees applying for open positions should go through a selection process similar to that of candidates from outside of the organization. The process will have some variation, as you should already have some knowledge about the candidates from their existing employee files and performance reviews; input can also be acquired from current managers and coworkers. As you evaluate performance and behavior, you will want to assess existing employees for talent and fit for the new role, too, since these things are at the core of world-class performance.

Internal candidates can be good options, because they are known by your organization and they know your organization back. Yet keep in mind the value of having a wide recruiting funnel at the start. Give yourself the best shot at finding the right talent for the role by being creative in who you attract through the search. And while it is natural to want to promote from within and allow growth potential, avoid the temptation to select the internal candidate simply because that person is a known entity in the right industry. It's important to evaluate whether they have the potential and talent capacity to enter the new role.

> **Give yourself the best shot at finding the right talent for the role by being creative in who you attract through the search.**

Too often I have seen a great employee promoted to a new role that ended up not being a good fit for that person. The bad fit tends to wear down the former star employee's ego and brand so much that the truly good employee ends up quitting. The person who is right for one role isn't necessarily right for another, yet sometimes you don't know until you try. I have a client who is very good at managing this uncertainty. They allow employees, if qualified, to try a new role, and they evaluate the employee within that new role at 30 days, 90 days, and 180 days to determine if it's a right fit. If not, and if the employees are still in good standing, the company allows them to reposition. Why the "still in good standing" comment? Sometimes you will see people start behaving differently because of their discomfort with the new role. And often the people acting out don't even realize they are doing it.

When you acknowledge the value of talent by building it into your selection process, you can have a greater rate of success from the start. Individuals will hit the ground running with the right passion, energy, and gifts to excel in the new role, and, once on the job, they can acquire additional skills, knowledge, and experience as needed.

Every job requires specific talent, and every person that you interview to fill that job has their own unique talent "footprint." In fact, as people, we are truly unique and special, which makes choosing someone for a job role messy. There is only a 1 in 275,000 chance that anyone who has taken the Clifton StrengthsFinder assessment will have the same top five strengths in any order. There is only a 1 in 33.4 million chance that anyone would have the exact same five strengths in the same order.[4] And that's just the top five key, leading strengths, let alone the unique combinations we see in people when we consider their thirty-four ranked strengths. Talent is a complex and powerful component of any high-performing employee. By creating a talent-based role profile that matches well to a given job opening, recruiting creatively, and screening well for the needed talent, the optimism often felt at the start of a new employee's job can be converted into performance that delivers world-class results for the organization.

6

YOU ONLY GET ONE FIRST DAY

Make a Good Impression While Onboarding and Training New Employees

By now, you are utilizing your human capital consciousness and tapping into it to hire the right person for the job and for your organization: right role, right person, right fit. Next up: onboarding and training that makes the employee feel valued and aligns with your business brand, strategy, leadership, and culture. When it comes to conscious onboarding and training, it all starts with the first day on the job. Consider the following.

- Lisa spends her first day on the job sitting at a desk with no computer. IT tells her that it will arrive in a week and that it could take several days for her e-mail address to be activated.

- Ben sits in an eight-hour new employee training session that consists entirely of videos and no human interaction.

- Susan receives an office tour from Clyde, a jaded administrative assistant who is set to retire in three months as the new leadership makes personnel changes to strengthen the company brand. While they make the rounds, Clyde informs her, in lascivious detail, about every scandal and misstep ever experienced by the company. By the time Susan gets back to her desk, she's wondering what she's gotten herself into.

How's that for a first day? Would you want any of these to be the first day for one of your employees? This is what I call onboarding without one's consciousness focused on human capital. Unfortunately, days like these are happening in organizations everywhere—not because companies don't care but because they don't realize how important the first day on the job really is or they are just too busy to consciously cultivate a first impression. It's time to get one's mind on human capital once again. You only get one first day with each new employee. If you seek world-class performance, you've got to make the first day count. It's time to create the onboarding experience with your consciousness engaged.

How do we go about creating a great first day on the job? There are so many ways. When I look at some of the larger companies, for example, they do amazing work online: welcome videos, online orientations that can be viewed before the first day, and welcome packets sent via email. Smaller companies may not have the resources for a high-tech welcome, but I have seen them create a great onboarding experience through an in-person meeting with the company founder or leaving welcome baskets of the new team members' favorite items and balloons on the new person's desk. How about the personal, handwritten welcome note from their leader or manager?

And don't forget to communicate this staffing change to other team members. Is it more awkward to find a stranger in the office or to be that stranger? Eliminate the uncomfortable "who's the new guy?" whispers from your new hire's first day by having the new employee fill out a "getting to know you" information sheet ahead of time that asks about his preferred name or nickname, hometown, alma mater, hobbies, likes, and interests (among other things); then distribute that information sheet along with your announcement of the new employee's imminent start date and role within the organization. That way, the team members know who is coming in and when and can be prepared with an icebreaking opening line that identifies something they have in common ("Welcome to the company, Fred! Guess what? I graduated from University of Kansas, too. Rock Chalk!").

The informational details of helping a new employee feel acclimated during onboarding are as important as the sentiment of "we care" that is expressed. Some organizations do an awesome job of making sure that executives are involved on the first day, whether it's through an in-person introduction or a video featuring one or more key executives that introduce these leaders and share the message of the culture. Familiarizing employees with leadership as soon as they walk through the doors says, "We value employees and relationships."

The onboarding and training period is also a key branding opportunity—a time to make solid first impressions and shape an employee's understanding of organizational culture from the start. When Disney runs new employees through their Traditions training, their brand of wonder and fun is felt from start to finish. According to one employee, the walls of the meeting room are covered with colorful Disney artwork and inspiring quotes, each employee finds a pair of mouse ears waiting at her place wrapped with red paper and a bow, and employees' names show up on the PowerPoint slides inside mouse-ear graphics. Training kicks off with trivia questions on Disney lore. Employees take a bus ride to Magic Kingdom to break up the training day and, when back at the meeting room, receive a surprise visit from Mickey himself.[1] How's that for branding, entertainment, and personalization? If your organization's brand is cutting edge, think about how to convey that in onboarding and training, from the interactive technology used to deliver training to the graphics used on the employee handouts. If

> Familiarizing employees with leadership as soon as they walk through the doors says, "We value employees and relationships."

your paperwork uses Courier font and looks like it was generated on a typewriter, you're sending mixed messages from the start.

There are as many ways to make a first day great for new employees as there are companies, and it will vary and depend on the size of the organization. Sometimes onboarding and training fall to HR, sometimes they fall to the business division. Either way, applying human capital consciousness to the equation can make all the difference in helping employees achieve their best performance.

This chapter will explore some key onboarding and training concepts that you can customize to your organization to ensure your onboarding and training procedures authentically welcome new employees into your organizational culture and engage them from the start. While I will throw in a few how-to's along the way, my goal is to steep you in the human capital consciousness philosophy as it applies to onboarding and training new employees and let you run from there.

BE OUR GUEST: ONBOARDING WITH A SENSE OF HOSPITALITY

When it comes to onboarding new employees, there's a balancing act between the mundane things that need doing and a positive first experience at the office. Yes, you need to convey important facts and information, but you also need to be conscious of how your new employees are going to experience this flood of information. While the policies of the organization and the layout of the building may be important to communicate, they aren't necessarily the most stimulating bodies of knowledge to share. (Does anyone get excited when handed a manual of legal policies or given a tour of the copy room?) With the right consciousness and a little work, the method by which you convey this knowledge creates an energizing first day. Think engagement, not overload.

WELCOME TO THE ORGANIZATION

Let's talk about onboarding as occurring across the following three areas:

- Compensation and benefits
- Policies and procedures
- Organizational culture

I'm sure that none of these items is a surprise to you. The key is the context in which you are providing this information. This is not some rote laundry list of facts that you bombard or overwhelm the employee with; it's a welcoming invitation for the new employee to step into the safety net of your organization. It's a way of saying, "Here's who we are, this is the family we are, and we want you to be successful. We look out for each other so we can all succeed together.

Compensation and Benefits

Let's look at compensation and benefits first. These are typically referred to as the benefits package, but I like to call it your Peace of Mind (POM) package. These are the ancillary things the organization puts into place for employees so they don't have to worry about them and can focus on meeting the expectations of the job. These include compensation, health insurance, personal time off, family/medical leave, retirement-savings matching, and the like. I look at the POM package as a way of saying, "We don't want you to be worrying about your health or your family; we want you to know that we are providing you the security you need so you can be your best self at work. You leverage your talents, skills, knowledge, experience, and values for us, and we will reward you and provide you with security for your efforts." That creates a much different experience for the employee than if she is coming to work worrying about things like, "I don't have an opportunity to save for retirement," or "What if something happens to my family?"

Policies and Procedures

Next up during onboarding is the familiar download of policies and procedures at the organization. You know that you've got to get your new people set up on e-mail. They need to get oriented to the technology they will be using regularly. They need to know who to contact for office supplies and how to submit requests for items that need to be reordered or for specialized equipment. How will the employee operate successfully in this environment? At Starbucks, every new employee at corporate learns how to pull espresso shots and check for quality. There's something to be said for learning hands-on. In what ways can you engage your employees in understanding policies and procedures in the real world, rather than throwing them a ten-thousand-page manual to fall asleep to?

Again, think deeper than the surface here. It's about more than just getting the computer and phone set up or inserting knowledge into your new employee's brain; it's about helping your new employee get comfortable maneuvering through your organization's system so her initial excitement at taking on the new job is sustained. It's about facilitating the employee's fit within the organization by welcoming her, educating her, and eliminating friction (see chapter 3 for more on fit). An engaging start, with as little friction as possible, sets up the employee for effective performance.

One thing to think about when you are creating your policies and procedures is what you want your culture to be and feel like. Do you want to hand new employees a single-spaced legal document detailing policies and procedures when you are working to create a fun and trusting environment? Now I know there is a balancing act involved in covering what's needed on the legal front in an engaging way, but many times the level of detail required is a bit overboard. Think about how to go over what needs conveying in a way that is the best fit for your culture.

When it comes to getting new employees oriented on their benefits as well as organizational policies and procedures, think of what the experience is like when you go on vacation and check into your favorite hotel room. Certain amenities are included, and the staff tell you about them so that you can avail yourself of the privileges. You are told, "Here's your room key, two bottles of water, fresh linens. Breakfast is from 6:00 a.m. to 10:00 a.m.," that kind of thing. Imagine the trouble you could run into if you didn't know the shuttle bus runs from 9:00 a.m. to 9:00 p.m. and taxis don't come out this far after 10:00 p.m. Think about creating the same friendly, high-quality, information-rich experience for your new employees as your organization onboards them. Different environment, same positive experience.

get your hands on...

CALL YOUR EMPLOYEES THE NAME THEY WANT TO BE CALLED

Does a Rose addressed by any other name feel just as sweet? I'm not sure: Maybe we should ask Rose. She might be happier being called Rosie or Rosanna, by her middle name, or by a nickname bestowed by her beloved *abuela*. Although such a courtesy as asking for someone's preferred name may seem intuitive, how many of us clarify with our employees the name by which they want to be called? Have you ever asked the question?

If a cultural value of your organization is showing respect for people as individuals and creating a relationship-based environment, this is a fabulous way to set the tone. During the selection process, check in with the applicant to see how he or she would like to be addressed. People usually put their legal, given names on résumés and job applications, as they do when registering for school and as they did at their previous places of employment. Using your given name is a good continuity strategy that makes it easier for your records and accomplishments to follow you, and it's a strategy that you've likely used too.

Yet, during day-to-day interactions with others, an employee may prefer to use another name. Charles may prefer Chuck. Patricia may go by Mary, her middle name. Melinda may go by Sunny, which is what her family calls her because of her bright and cheerful disposition (it's no wonder you hired her)! John Smith III may go by Trey. I have a client who goes by IV, as in Ivy, because he was the fourth male descendent of his name: IV. If you want someone to turn around when you say his name, find out which name is most likely to get the reaction you seek!

Also take this personalization a step further: Make sure the office placard, business cards, stationery, e-mail addresses, and directory listings all use the employee's preferred name. If a coworker is trying to find Trey, he's going to walk right past John's office. If a customer is trying to send an e-mail to the very helpful Sunny to discuss some new business but the only person with that last name on the website is Melinda, that customer is going to think Sunny's left for greener pastures.

You value your employees, so make them feel valued. One of the easiest ways to do so is to call them what they want to be called.

Organizational Culture

Compensation and benefits, policies and procedures—with each and every step you take to ease your new employee into learning this new information, you are simultaneously teaching him or her about your organizational culture. The Human Capital Optimization Model requires you to be conscious about educating new employees on your organization's culture. This education doesn't occur willy-nilly, haphazardly, or de facto; it occurs by design. Every interaction with your newly hired employees is an opportunity to engage (or disengage) new employees in the organizational culture.

From the start, you can orient employees to the big picture of what the organization feels like—this is what we are about and what our expectations are. This is how we dress; this is what's acceptable behavior; it's critical that you join in the once-a-month lunch, as that's where you learn about the most recent activities going on in the organization.

So how do you go about teaching some of that content up front versus having the employees just learn as they go? Of course, your new hires will pick up on how things work at your organization haphazardly over time, but if you can have some fun case studies, trivia games, or employees who would like to share their experiences with the new team members in a lunch group panel called The Things You Might Want to Know but Don't Want to Ask, go with the creative, fun, or social way to get your message across and set your new employees on the fast track to engagement.

Again, keep your brand in mind when introducing new employees to your organizational culture. If yours is a relationship business, make sure your organization's leaders come and introduce themselves during orientation. Take new employees out to dinner with others on their team, or host a cocktail party. If you have an organization that's a bit more entrepreneurial and people are to figure things out on their own, one way that I like to help get new employees to connect with others and get oriented to organizational procedures and culture is to send them on a scavenger hunt. To make the process practical and fun, we give them a list of people that the employee should meet and places he or she should know. Where do you go to get extra uniforms? Who puts in software orders? Here are eight people to meet—set up thirty-minute meetings with each to learn what they do. Getting your employee embedded very quickly gets your employee engaged quickly too.

WELCOME TO THE NEW ROLE

After the download has been done for the employee on compensation, benefits, policies, procedures, and organizational culture, it's time for *role training*. Remember all that time your team spent on developing the right job role profile? The role profile should continue to get utilized during onboarding and training. The manager in charge of the new employee and the new employee himself are probably quite happy that the job role is filled, but do they both know what precisely the new hire is going to be doing? This is what role training is about.

Although the job role may be clear in the manager's mind, the new employee may have applied to a dozen other jobs at the same time as she submitted an application for yours. In the hubbub of the switch from an old job to the new job in your organization, she might have forgotten some of the details of this specific role. What is she responsible for? What will the schedule be like? What supports are already in place and how can they be accessed? What does the first month look like? Role training is an important part of the onboarding experience as it sets the individual up to do the right job. Role training is also an essential part of the performance management process (see chapter 8); it is the first step in making sure that employees know what they are supposed to be doing so they can be given feedback and held accountable for their role

> **Many times when expectations go astray, it's because the amount of time an employee spent on a particular job duty may be different than his manager expected.**

down the line. It enables the kind of fine-tuning and achievement of goals that leads to world-class performance.

One key area to cover is time allocation. Many times when expectations go astray, it's because the amount of time an employee spent on a particular job duty may be different than his manager expected. The manager and new employee should review and discuss the job description together to make sure they're both on the same page. That's human capital consciousness—doing all you can to ensure that the employee aligns to the desired role.

TRAINING FOR DIFFERENT LEARNING STYLES

If you've hired right, your employee has got talent; now it's time to make sure your new employee has the skills and knowledge needed to jump into the job and start moving. As your organization provides training, be cognizant of learning styles and of timing. You don't want to do the same thing in the same place the whole time, like sitting in the classroom for five days a week, eight hours a day. You want to create an environment of variety. After going through the talent-based selection process with this employee, you should have a good sense of her learning style. If not, speak to the recruiter and HR to bridge the gap. Be aware of how your employee learns and tailor the training accordingly. Some people need to read the handbook before jumping into training. Some do better learning on the fly. Others actually benefit from classroom-style instruction.

There is often a gap between the information on learning style already known about a new employee and the type of training provided to that person. The first reason this gap exists is that the individuals who select a person for a job are not your trainers, so, if you can, have the HR professional, the trainer, and the manager sit down and exchange this information. Another option would be to start building an online repository of information about a candidate during the application process so that people down line can draw from the knowledge gained by predecessors who have worked with the candidate-turned-employee and then add to it.

Good trainers should be able to read information about a person and then translate that information into the best teaching style to use with this individual. It is critically important to understand who the person is if that person's training experience is to be maximized. Too often we spend money and time on selection tools or have that information on the candidate, and then it doesn't get shared.

You may be thinking, "Ugh! I don't have time to customize training to each individual employee!" Well, guess what? If you don't customize now, you may end up wasting the time you spend offering a one-size-fits-all training module, because your employee may not get the message and will need to be retrained in his specific style down the line when it's clear he hasn't grasped the material and can't perform as needed. Or your employee may think that the failure to absorb the lesson is her fault and leave the organization under the assumption that she wasn't really cut out for the position.

Think about the customized training this way: If you're going to grow a garden, you need to cultivate the soil, but you need to enrich the soil in a way that's crop specific. Your garden is not going to produce great strawberries when you've prepared the ground for cabbage. Help get new employees with different learning styles engaged at a high level, consistently, when they're first starting their job by personalizing training with their specific learning styles in mind.

Figure 6.1: Human Capital Optimization Model Close-Up:
Selecting, Hiring, and Onboarding New Employees

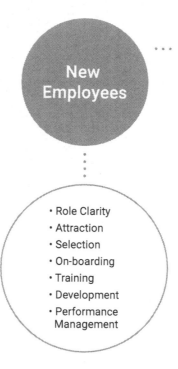

New
Employees

- Role Clarity
- Attraction
- Selection
- On-boarding
- Training
- Development
- Performance
  Management

more to get your mind on...

FIRST-DAY CHECKLIST

As I've said many times, the organization has
only one first day with a new employee; make a
good impression! You also have a lot of work to do to get your
employee up to speed. To see a checklist of things your team
may need to go over with your new hire, visit www.loristohs
.com/getyourmindon.

CONCLUSION: ONBOARDING AND TRAINING AS A LAUNCHING PAD TO WORLD-CLASS PERFORMANCE

At the core of my philosophy of effective onboarding and training is this: engage, align, and brand. If your culture and brand revolve around innovative design and modern style, expose new employees to that from the get-go: let them touch and feel your latest products, see your sense of design embedded in the training room and PowerPoint slides, and try their own hand at capturing your brand by competing in a mock design contest.

If your brand is one of historical preservation and safeguarding of traditions, provide a well-done video that tells the story of the organization's rich past, provide manuals in classic leather binders with monogramming, and invite old-timers to lunch to share engaging stories about organizational traditions and lore.

With a little creativity and strategic thinking, the options for creative onboarding and training activities are plentiful. If you can welcome new employees into your organizational practices and culture with a sense of energy versus apathy, you will have successfully bridged the hiring stage to the performance stage. Add in time spent getting super clear on the new job role, and new employees will have the valuable information and expectations they need to help them perform at a world-class level.

You likely have big goals and dreams for the organizational brand as a leader, and you may wonder where the ideals of the brand and the culture sometimes get lost. Well, sometimes it's the small things that matter when aligning employees to the brand,

and the enculturation needs to start on day one. Get started on the right foot by, even on that very first day, aiming to create a nice mix of activities that keeps things interesting while covering all the key components for the employee: compensation and benefits, policies and procedures, organizational culture, and training for their core role. Be mindful of learning styles, and customize the onboarding and training experience for each new hire.

Using onboarding as an opportunity to engage new employees and welcome them into your brand takes engagement to the next level—one that gets employees grounded from the start in the organization's culture and values. That approach turns onboarding and training from mundane drudgery to a launching pad to the high performance and execution of organizational strategy that comes from strong employee engagement.

Go big on the first day. You only get one chance.

PART III

get your mind on...
MANAGING

"When I grow up, I want to be a manager," said no one.

7

MANAGING FOR
WORLD-CLASS PERFORMANCE

"What do you want to be when you grow up?"

Do you remember how you answered that question long ago? Each of us has our own unique answer to that question when we are kids. Yet, there is one answer you do not hear from young people. "When I grow up, I want to be a manager!"

Is it any surprise? It's a job more often satirized than glorified by Hollywood. It's a job not often in the spotlight, unless something goes terribly wrong. The people who do this job well are essential to the engagement of the people they manage and the success of the business that employs them, yet if a manager is truly doing his job well, people outside the organization don't know the manager's name.

Once in a while you will have someone who is a great example of a manager—and it's so great to see!—but, unfortunately, that's not a common occurrence. Those who end up in the management role often get there simply because they are great at their technical skill or knowledgeable about the role, not necessarily because they love managing people. Those who take on the manager role with excitement may quickly discover how hard it is to develop people when they

> **Those who end up in the management role often get there because they are great at their technical skill or knowledgeable about the role, not because they love managing people.**

have too much other work on their plates—the tangible tasks and deadlines of "real work." Then there is the fact that managing people is a messy business. People aren't robots that managers can simply program; they are dynamic beings who need support and attention. If management is unglamorous from the outside looking in, it's even less glamorous from deep inside the trenches. Yet, we have to get management right! With your consciousness about human capital awakened, you know it's important to put the right people in the right roles. This applies not just to the line jobs, but to managers as well.

Glamorous or no, the role of the manager is critical to the success of any organization. Great managers drive great performance; poor managers often drive employees into the ground and then away. Engaged teams, in which good managers are the heart, show less turnover (24 percent to 59 percent), higher customer ratings (10 percent), and greater profitability (21 percent) than do disengaged teams. They also show higher productivity (17 percent), less shrinkage (28 percent), fewer safety incidents (70 percent!), and less absenteeism (41 percent).[1]

Businesses that have gone the extra mile to maximize their employee engagement have seen their earnings per share achieve values 147 percent higher than those of their competitors.[2] Talented managers who double the rate of employee engagement can make such gains happen, according to *Gallup Business Journal.*[3] Flip that around, and the picture for disengaged teams isn't pretty. Good managers and their consequently engaged employees lead to enviable performance that any leader would want to attain for her organization.

In addition to leading to great performance, great management is important because it ensures that the talent you hire stays in place and flourishes rather than walks away. The fact of the matter is, much of the time, employees don't leave organizations; they leave managers. So you may have the most talented, skilled, knowledgeable, and experienced employees on the planet—ones who click with your organizational values and culture—but if you put these individuals to work for bad managers, they are sure to drift away over time.

Notice that I'm talking about individuals. Groups of people can get tagged with the "difficult to manage" label. Take, for example, the management scapegoats du jour, millennials. "They" (whoever "they" may be) say that millennials are management challenges because they want attention, they want feedback, and they are not afraid to ask for it, repeatedly. If they don't get the feedback and attention they desire, so it is said, millennials are less inclined to stay. Yet this generation, like any generation, is made up of individuals who need to be treated as such.

Sure, a millennial may leave your workplace, but the separation may be through disengagement, departure from the department they've been groomed to support, or, worse yet, an exit from the organization, and the reason for the departure will be specific to that individual's situation, not to the generation or group that individual comes from or is associated with. Regardless, the end result is the same: there goes your valuable human capital. Lost training time. Lost productivity. Lost talent. Lost dollars. Low-quality deliverables. Less engaged customers. You name it. Clearly, that's not how we intend to build our organizations.

THE PROBLEM: MANAGERS WHO REALLY SHOULDN'T BE MANAGING

It's a common refrain: "I love my job, but, well, I wish I had a different manager." As I prepare for speaking engagements that are part of my client management programs, I typically reach out to a sampling of the client's managers' direct reports and make one simple request: "Please complete this sentence: I wish my manager would

_____." Now, I must say that a small percentage of people say, "Keep doing what they are doing." For the most part, though, the blank gets filled in with phrases that indicate something is lacking, phrases like, "Tell me how I am doing," "Let me do my job," "Be clear on what he/she expects from me," "Treat me with respect," or some other simple yet unfulfilled request. These requests are straightforward but important. When left unaddressed, these behaviors your employees wish would change start to grind on your people, drumming the engagement right out of them. Far too many talented people in organizations today become miserable and disengaged on the job because of their manager.

Now, we could chalk this up as an employee attitude problem, but the dysfunction runs deeper than that. Sure, some employees would do well to look within rather than blame their managers for discontent on the job, but more often the problem we see is truly one of poor management. I don't think that anyone has the intention of being a bad manager, but we as organizations need to take a look inside and see how we can do a better job at choosing our managers and setting them up for success.

Let's first look at selecting the right managers. According to research by Gallup, people with the talent to manage number only about one in ten.[4] No wonder it's hard to find good managers. The

> **According to research by Gallup, people with the talent to manage number only about one in ten.**

trickiest reality is that poor management does not necessarily occur because the person in the management role is "bad" in some wholesale way but because the organization lacks the fundamental framework needed to hire the right people for management and then set them up for success with the right employee performance management process (see chapter 8).

We've all seen the disappointing case of a good employee or promising candidate turned into a frightening manager (who, at the very least, causes his direct reports to lose more than a little sleep). It's a painful sight that we may not fully understand and that leaves us scratching our heads in confusion, with comments like

- "But she interviewed so well!"
- "He was a fantastic performer in all of his past roles. What happened?"
- "We gave her so much time and training, but she still can't manage well. What is going on?"

These perfectly nice and once high-performing individuals, when promoted to a management role, have flopped. "That wasn't supposed to happen!" Key to remember, though, is that while the management performance itself may have been a flop, the candidates themselves are probably not: in all likelihood, they are just not a fit for the management role. To address this issue once and for all, we need to step back and think about what we are seeking in candidates for the management role. It's all about finding the right human capital for the job!

HIRING RIGHT: DO YOU REALLY WANT TO BE A MANAGER WHEN YOU GROW UP?

When I think about how best to fill the role of manager within an organization or department, I think of the following story. At one of my client sales meetings, several of the salespeople came up to me to ask about the sales manager positions that were expected to be coming open soon. Many of them wanted to put a bug in my ear and let me know that they were interested in being considered for the role. So at that moment, during the casual conversation and chitchat, I asked, "Why do you want to be a manager?"

As I listened, I realized that their answers were consistently more about achieving a different lifestyle—fewer hours, higher pay, more prestige—rather than about a genuine interest in investing in people. Yet that's what a true manager is: a person who cares about others being successful, knocking barriers out of their way and enabling them to succeed. I must say I got a few answers along those altruistic lines, but most responses were more about bettering themselves or their situation, not about helping others. Up went the red flag!

If someone is a salesperson or a star performer in his field, that person is used to being the lead in the show. That's why we hire people like that for sales. In a management role, individual star performers are no longer the knight on the horse anymore, charging in to save the day. Instead, they're sitting back, developing each member of the team into a star performer, and playing an important but ultimately more humble role. Like a parent, a manager nurtures others, helping people grow without much glory coming back to the manager (but taking plenty of blame if things go wrong)! Although they are not out there in droves, we have to work to find the great sales performer who has the management talent and desire to invest in others. We've got to find the right human capital for the role.

Where does the ability to be a good manager come from? While you may say it comes from experience, yes, experience helps, but when those with great experience were studied, they had another key component: talent. Good management comes from talent! The raw talents for management exist within the people who do well with this job, from understanding that each person is unique, to helping a person to strategize, to finding ways to help him to grow and expand, to watching out for his best interests.

When I am helping to hire for management roles, we define clearly what talents a manager needs to have and then we determine whether the candidate is a right fit. Here are some red flags to watch for when selecting the right talent for a management role, as well as the green flags that you can try to shift to, to remedy the situation.

Table 7.1: Turning Red Flags into Green Flags: Dealing with Someone Who May or May Not Be a Good Candidate for a Manager Role

Red Flag	What's the Problem?	Green Flag
More Pay! You ask someone applying for a management job why he wants to be a manager and he says he is seeking a higher salary and better hours.	Although fair pay and work-life balance may be important to a great manager, a good potential manager is motivated by the desire to help and support others in their performance and professional development, not seeking the role just to get better pay and hours.	If someone cites money or time as the reason he is interested in management, dig deeper to find out what natural talent he has around managing people, as well as his managerially relevant skills, knowledge, and experience.
Superstar Status You think, "This person is a superstar at IT/sales/whatever. Let's promote this stellar employee to manage our IT/sales/whatever team."	What makes someone great in her field does not necessarily make that person great at being a manager.	Before promoting a superstar to management, make sure that person has the talent to understand the team members personally— their strengths, experience, talents, motivations, and so on.— and figure out how to delegate the department's work to the right people.
Gotta Get Results The candidate says, "I love getting results and producing at a high level of performance."	High performers often get their motivation from achieving results, especially if they are paid for performance, but to be a good manager, a person needs to be willing to support other people in getting results.	Make sure the candidate is going to be able to trade the adrenaline rush of nailing project work for the slower burn of developing star employees. They have to be able to teach others to fish and not fish for them.

How can we turn these red flags into green flags that bring success? The Whole Person Model, introduced in chapter 3 (see Figure 3.1), holds the key. To review, when hiring, we need to seek candidates (whether internal or external) who have the talent, skills, knowledge, experience, and values to succeed in the role of manager. Let's look at talent closely, because that can't be taught and needs to be possessed from the start.

Those who have talent for management have an innate capacity to manage people well by working closely with them to develop their strengths, providing feedback, and holding them accountable. When I talk about having a talent for management, I am referring to things like being able to tell people hard truths without beating them down or making them feel discouraged, being able to multitask and manage multiple people's issues and projects at the same time, and having the insight to see past a roadblock to get at the true heart of an employee's problem.

It helps, of course, if the manager has talents that allow her to understand, if not do, the job her team is assigned to complete; but management is only tangentially about that assigned job at hand. Remember, the manager is not in place to do the team's assigned work; the manager is in place to ensure the team completes the assigned work to the best of their combined talents and abilities. The manager's work is the team, and the manager's talents should reflect the focus on her people.

No matter how much we all agree that when you're hiring for management that you need someone who is a good fit for the role, the real issue is that the organization is not starting from scratch. Many of the management roles are already filled—with people who shouldn't be managing!

Without even realizing it, many leaders have allowed their organizations to become infiltrated by managers who were promoted from within because they were great in their fields (but not necessarily at managing people) or by those who applied from outside the organization and convinced someone they were ready to make the leap to management because of industry experience without being assessed for the innate talent to manage. So the wrong people are being picked for management, and then we are surprised when they don't perform that well as managers. (Learn more about how to fix the problem of underperforming managers in the "Capitalizing on the Talents of the Manager and Learning to Fill the Gaps" section later in this chapter as well as in chapter 8.)

> **Many leaders have allowed their organizations to become infiltrated by managers who were promoted from within because they were great in their fields (but not necessarily at managing people).**

It's a recipe for low-performance managers: people lack the interest or innate talent to manage, so they avoid developing people at all costs. As long as their roles are structured to allow them to be coach-player roles, they will have every excuse to get their tangible work completed and let the people management stuff fall to the bottom of the list of priorities. Yet, setting up successful management can transform a department.

Take, for example, the situation Belinda, the director of a non-profit, found herself in while overseeing the work of Mary, a manager with the title of fundraising development director. Mary was a wonderful person, but resource development was not one of her talents. Also not a talent? Setting strategy. Yet, these were the two primary talents the job required of Mary for successful completion.

Mary was a wonderful person and a hard worker, but she was unable to develop an effective strategy and deploy her people to execute it, so her team was floundering. Eventually, Mary ended up leaving the organization, and Belinda was able to select a person with greater innate talents for the position. With Mary gone and the new employee functioning well in the position, Belinda was amazed to discover the surplus of time and energy she now had to devote to her own job.

That's the thing. If one manager is not functioning well in her position, that often means that manager's manager is picking up the slack, either by doing that person's job in the hopes that the struggling manager will learn from the demonstration or by training the manager over and over again, in the hopes that one of the training sessions will eventually stick. Once a low-functioning manager has transitioned out of the position and someone with a better fit for the role has transitioned in, the manager's manager can go back to doing his job alone, time now free to do what he does best. When the right people with the right talents take on the right roles, the whole organization will be the better for it. Individual performers stay engaged as do their managers. Your human capital remains alive and awake!

---

more to get your mind on...

DON'T LET PROJECT WORK EAT YOUR MANAGERS!

Getting the right people in the role of management is essential. Once they are there, then what? Another principle to ensure effective management is to avoid overloading your managers with project work, making them too busy to actually manage or simply giving them an excuse not to. Too many employee-focused management roles have shifted to working manager roles. That's an organizational problem—making people do more with less—but it also allows people who don't like to manage people to avoid that part of the job and lose themselves in the work. To learn how to combat this tendency, visit www.loristohs.com/getyourmindon for more.

USING STRENGTHS TO FOSTER WORLD-CLASS PERFORMANCE

The journey to great management also includes an ability on the part of the manager to understand and leverage strengths—one's own as well as one's people's. While certain talents, skills, and values must be there for a person to succeed at management, there's no need to expect a manager to have every single strength and talent that might be good for the role. If the essential criteria are there, the rest can be complemented. Knowing how to do this can turn around a less than satisfactory management performance for a manager who is already in place or help set up a new manager and his team for success from the start.

Capitalizing on the Talents of the Manager and Learning to Fill the Gaps

Josh and Jennifer were both managers in the Business Development Department of a digital media company. When it came to light how much better Josh's team's numbers were, we began to investigate the differences in Josh's versus Jennifer's management styles to see if we could help her improve her own team's productivity.

Through a study of his employees, we discovered that what made Josh so great as a manager was his naturally engaging style with his people. Josh did not hide in his office or bury himself in project work. Instead, he regularly interacted with his people. He asked them how things were going, he gave them ideas, he made himself available, and he encouraged them. He gave them the individualized attention they each desired by checking in with them.

When team members set goals and didn't reach them, Josh felt comfortable asking what their challenges were. Because he was so engaged during earlier stages of brainstorming and action, it felt natural to simply follow up. This worked well given the trust that existed between him and his people. They knew when he checked in on progress and asked about outcomes, he genuinely cared about their success and the success of the team. He wasn't being an arrogant leader demanding results just so he looked good.

In contrast, Jill was more stand-offish than Josh by nature. She loved her people just as much as Josh loved his, but given her more reserved personality, she did not feel motivated to walk the halls of the office and talk as regularly to her team members. She was comfortable with one-on-one meetings, which was good, but when she had them, she found it hard to hold her people accountable for the work she had asked them to do. Jill was uncomfortable with conflict, and this made it hard for her to talk with employees directly about why they had not met certain goals and expectations.

When we dug deeper, we realized in concert with Jill that she needed to do a better job of being clear on expectations with her people at the start of each project—deliverables, timelines, and the like. This gave her the comfort level needed to check on where things had gone off track because she knew she would not be blindsiding her employees but rather circling back on conversations they had already had. During those initial expectation-setting conversations, Jill also learned to be clear that these regular check-ins were conducted to support the employee in his and her growth because she cared about the employee and wanted to see him or her succeed. She knew that when her employees did well, the department did well, and that these results were a win for everyone.

As was the case for Josh and Jill, every manager brings a set of unique strengths and talents to the role. While these strengths and talents all need to be applied to a performance management process that

> **The key is to set clear expectations on the outcomes and be aware of each manager's unique style so he or she can create processes to accommodate gaps.**

includes consistent elements such as setting expectations, holding people accountable, and providing feedback (described in the next chapter in more detail), variability in management style is okay. It's as variable as we are human.

The key is to set clear expectations on the outcomes and be aware of each manager's unique style so he or she can create processes to accommodate gaps. This may involve tweaking how the manager engages in performance management, as Jill did with her initial expectation setting, or pulling in another team member to fill in a manager's blind spots. Know yourself the best, surround yourself with the rest. We all need good partners.

A manager with less of an ability to read emotions might ask a team member with a sharp EQ and high empathy to be charged with letting the manager know when employee emotions are starting to run high around an issue. A manager with high responsibility who does the assigned work quickly and struggles to delegate may need to step back, teach the direct reports, and be patient with learning so the manager is not enabling the employees to slack off by doing the work for them.

Managing the Strengths of the Team

Just as effective managers know their own strengths and how to adjust for gaps in their skill sets, managers need to be clear, too, on each of their team member's strengths and how to use them. The challenge is how best to align the talents of one's employees with the strategy the team is being charged with executing.

It's great to have a team at one's disposal when staring at a massive plan that needs to be put into action. However, the manager needs to take a moment to strategize before starting to sling assignments around to whoever's available to handle them. Assessing who is most adept at doing what—whose talents align with the work that needs to be done—and assigning work accordingly is what elevates the team from acceptable to world class.

Leadership researcher and speaker Marcus Buckingham says that "average managers play checkers, while great managers play chess."[5] What does he mean? In checkers, you're moving around multiple pieces to achieve your goal of winning the game, but most of the time, each piece is interchangeable, indistinguishable, and, occasionally, easily sacrificed. In chess, different rules govern the moves of each piece, and the best players think multiple moves ahead. The strategy a chess player executes depends in large part on what the individual pieces can do, and great chess players, like great managers, harness the individual characteristics of the pieces to their own advantage.

Buckingham illustrates the point by discussing managers at Walgreens stores who have achieved remarkable results by capitalizing on the quirks and talents of individual employees. One Walgreens employee with a Goth look and a willingness to take the overnight shift turned out to be excellent at resets and revisions—essentially, restocking and arranging merchandise to specific company standards. If he was given general work assignments—"straighten the merchandise"—he wouldn't achieve much. But when given the binder full of directions for product placement and arrangement from corporate he would execute it to a profit-churning T. His manager recognized and positively reinforced his contributions and rearranged the usual way of doing things (which divided resets and revisions among many employees) to take advantage of this talent, handing him the R&R book and having him do it all (which he could do in record time, this being a talent of his).

As the employee's talent-based success increased his confidence, he asked to move to management. While his manager was initially hesitant to do so, he came up with a creative solution. He kept the store's ability to benefit from his natural talent and provided the employee with a new challenge by crafting a role that kept this employee doing revisions as an assistant manager while reassigning resets to another employee with a strong talent for arranging merchandise.[6]

A manager of another Walgreens store noticed that one of his employees thrived in competitive situations. Month after month, she crushed corporate monthly selling challenges, even while working the low-trafficked overnight shift. Her manager further noted that this employee's competitiveness was made even more acute by public recognition. In response, he dedicated the walls of the back office to tracking the store's sales on charts and figures, with the outstanding contributions of individual employees highlighted in red. His star performer gets to see her record-breaking sales on display for all who enter the office, something she appreciates so much she'll come in on her days off to check her numbers. Because this manager also recognizes the indi-

In both of these Walgreens stores, the secret of the managers' success is their willingness to recognize, work with, and maximize the talents of each employee on an individual basis.

vidual strengths of other employees in personalized ways, there's not the level of resentment you'd expect from her coworkers. It also certainly doesn't hurt that largely due to this employee's efforts, their store was ranked number one of all Walgreens for the suggestive selling program.[7]

In both of these Walgreens stores, the secret of the managers' success is their willingness to recognize, work with, and maximize the talents of each employee on an individual basis. This lesson can be translated to any workplace by making sure managers consider every member of the team and who they are as individuals when handing out assignments.

There's a bonus in all of this, too, in terms of keeping the manager engaged. Managing is much more rewarding when you have the right people doing the right work. It's fun to see someone thrive in a position as a result of one's management and coaching. That creates a consistent feedback loop that reinforces the manager's will to engage. Reread chapters 4 and 5 to review how to hire for the best fit for the job roles in your organization. Know and live those hiring and selecting methods, because they are essential to the success of the individual employees, the managers working with them, and ultimately your organization.

get your hands on...

SELECTING THE RIGHT
MANAGER FOR THE ROLE

Clearly, selecting the right manager for a given management role is essential to maximize the performance of your employees and, by extension, the success of your organization. How do you put the right person into the manager role?

To make sure your candidate has the right talent for management:

- Write an accurate role profile for the management position.
- Understand the candidate's motivation for applying for a management position and listen for key move-ahead phrases and red flags.

Sample move-ahead phrases:

- Interested in developing people
- Loves watching people grow
- Wants to apply team-building skills
- Passionate about collaboration and development

Sample red flags:

- In it for a lifestyle change (e.g., more money and prestige)
- In it for her own glorification
- Wants to "take the next step" in his career or in the office hierarchy
- Other reasons not having to do with a desire to help people develop and achieve their potential

Finally, to ensure the manager has time budgeted to develop her employees:

- Consider what constitutes a reasonable split of time and responsibilities between projects and people.
- Be flexible and keep communication open.
- Make sure, if you are managing managers, you model great management behavior.

Once you have all of these principles and responsibilities in mind for your manager, go to the Whole Person Model (see Figure 3.1 in chapter 3). Determine what you need in a manager in terms of skills, knowledge, experience, talent, and values to successfully fill this role. Then hire accordingly.

Once your candidate is in the position, be sure to onboard and train effectively. Then provide the ongoing support and direction your manager needs to succeed. After all, a manager's success means many other people—employees and customers alike—are also being rewarded with guidance and service. When everyone is engaged, your workplace will thrive.

MOVING FROM GOOD TO GREAT TO WORLD CLASS

Many organizations can be good, but to have performance that is world class, that is where the details come in. The right talent at the individual performer level mixed with the right talent at the management level can be the power factor that pushes organizations from good to great, to borrow a line from Jim Collins.

Bottom line: World-class performance doesn't have to be a mystery. No longer do we need to scratch our heads and wonder why it is that one work group excels over another when they both receive the same resources, training, store layout, products, services, et cetera. Why is one knocking it out of the park when another is doing just okay? Yes, geographical differences may matter, but at the end of the day, world-class performance comes from the great manager who inspires his people, understands them, and motivates them.

As I've already said, part-time talent doesn't make world-class performance. Full-time talent does, in team members and the manager who is orchestrating them to deliver on organizational strategy. This is the goal of the Human Capital Optimization Model: to fill a workplace with talented people who are enabled by engaged managers to put their talents to optimal, energizing use in pursuit of the organization's mission. When you are truly working the Human Capital Optimization Model, you will see changes in your people and your

> **Part-time talent doesn't make world-class performance.**

workplace over time: increased engagement, enhanced productivity, and a mind-set shift. Work will become energizing instead of draining. If all really goes to plan, work will hardly feel like work! This positive application of time and talent will also show in the organization's output and satisfied customers.

CONCLUSION: WHAT YOUR PEOPLE CAN ACHIEVE

An organization is nothing without its people. An organization is an idea, but without people to carry out its mission, there's not much to it except perhaps four walls and a lonely mission statement hanging on one of them. The power of an organization lies in what its people can achieve. Each person has potential that can be tapped into and linked back to the work, and if your organization's managers do so mindfully, recognizing the gifts of each individual and how they match up with the needs that must be met in the workplace, that link strengthens both the person and the organization. With the day-to-day, month-to-month, and quarter-to-quarter performance management strategies that follow in the next chapter, there's really no stopping your organization's impact on the market and the world.

There is so much talk today about what is the best performance management system. What should you do? What shouldn't you do?

STRENGTHS-BASED
PERFORMANCE MANAGEMENT

Building, building, and more building. If you've been working the Human Capital Optimization Model thus far, much of the people scaffolding of your organization is now in place. Job roles have been clearly defined so that they include the talent needed for the role. Individual performers have been hired for the right roles. Good managers, with identifiable management talent, are in place. The glue that keeps that people scaffolding together is performance management: the day-to-day, week-to-week, month-to-month, and year-to-year efforts by managers to guide their people to continually execute the organizational strategy through their roles and deliver desired outcomes.

A manager who is engaging in effective performance management is not so unlike the talented maestro conducting an orchestra. While the maestro never picks up an instrument, he is responsible for making beautiful music by coordinating the talented group of musicians who perform in sync due only to the conductor. How does he do this? Through his coaching during rehearsal and his gestures during the show: in short, through communication.

The superb manager, with a head full of insight into each of her employees—from their strengths and weaknesses to their current challenges and successes—is also able to conduct the team to create powerful outcomes together. The manager has a read on the individual team members, holds organizational strategy in mind, and guides individual contributors to perform at their best to create an integrated effort that delivers desired results. This guidance begins and ends with effective communication.

Performance management involves all of the things a manager does throughout the course of the year to help her people perform at their very best—fulfilling expectations, meeting goals, and delivering outcomes. It culminates with the measurement of performance outcomes, too, examining the degree to which goals have been met as well as whether employees and customers are engaged.

There is so much talk today about what is the best performance management system. What should you do? What shouldn't you do? Is it annual? Is it monthly? Is it a five-page complete review? Is it an online pulse survey? One thing I will say is consistent among performance management systems is that they involve continual care and feeding—continual attention and communication. While your organization may have a process that you believe in or not or that is cutting edge, performance management is best when it is consistent and fluid. After all, if you've saved up your performance critique all year for your employee's annual performance review, you've potentially had an employee working suboptimally over the year—or worse.

> **What people forget is that a fit that's not good for the organization is also often not good for the employee either.**

An organization I consulted for had an employee named Brett, who had been with them for seven years. He was known and liked for the person he was throughout the organization, which was great for in-office dynamics, but his performance was slipping and had been for years. Clearly, Brett's job role was not a fit for him anymore. Yet management held back. This was Brett! Everyone loved Brett. How could anyone sit this beloved employee down and say, "Buddy, we've got to be frank: you need to get back on track or we're going to need to part ways"?

It took a tremendously long time for someone to find the guts to step up and have the tough conversation, and by that point, no course correction would save Brett's job: the parting of ways was a certainty. When Brett received the news that he was being let go, he looked—relieved! He confessed that he'd been checked out—disengaged—from his job for at least three years. Letting him go was a mercy: Brett hadn't wanted to let the organization down by leaving, and now he was free to do so.

What happened here? First, it's understood that criticism can be hard to share with someone. Further, managers don't like to let people go, because they respect their employees and hate to part ways. Yet, it's the job of a manager to keep their people on task and on track and, if all else fails, to end unfruitful employment arrangements. What people forget is that a fit that's not good for the organization *is also often not good for the employee either.* Yet the employee has very little reason to sever the employment connection. A voluntary departure means no unemployment benefits, for example.

A manager's goal can be to avoid allowing an employment situation to get to this point. If someone had talked to Brett when his performance first started to suffer, perhaps he could have been coached back to peak performance, or perhaps he could have been moved to a new and more appropriate job role. Because no one communicated with Brett, three years of Brett's career and the organization's investment in Brett for this job role were wasted.

Effective performance management involves continual feedback, organic check-ins, and regular conversations that emerge from a manager who is in tune with his people, walking around the office and having meetings to ask questions, listen, brainstorm, and inspire. An engaged, performance-supporting manager constantly takes the pulse of her people, asking questions and making observations like the following:

- "How are *you?*" (Yes, I said, "How are *you?*" not just "How's the work going?")
- "What are you focusing on this week?"
- "What can I do to support you?"
- "You did great on the assignment for XYZ. What made it great for you?"
- "I notice you weren't able to get that report in on time. What's going on for you?"
- "I know you're really good at X, and I noticed that Jon could use someone good at X on his team. Are you interested in contributing?"
- "It seems like you're struggling with Y. Cara is a whiz at that and has offered to pitch in. What are your thoughts? Would you like her assistance?"

Although every manager will have his own style of managing people's work, effective management has the following component across the board: *consistent touch points and communication* between the manager and his people. Periodic conversations consciously created by the manager to tune in to key performance issues with employees are the heart of effective performance management. What's consistent? Weekly is optimal. That doesn't mean for hours, but we all know if we aren't in touch with our team members and time goes on, there's usually something to reign back in. If all is going well, then great, it's going well but there will be no unexpected surprises. Each weekly conversation adds up to a year of tracking to make sure there is alignment in the work and expectations. While the goal is to create a comfortable and trustworthy communication channel that feels natural and spontaneous, managers can use the structure suggested in this chapter to consciously create that culture of improvement and fine-tuning.

THE HEART OF PERFORMANCE MANAGEMENT: COMMUNICATION

When I bring up this idea of talking to one's people as a key part of the performance management process, managers often say to me, "I talk to my people all the time." In other words: *Been there. Done that.* My question to them is this: When you talk to your people, what is the content of the dialogue? Oftentimes, managers are having conversations with their employees about the nuts and bolts of their project work—client updates, production timelines, supply chain issues, and so on—and this is necessary and valuable. But let's not mistake those conversations with the kind of communication that needs to happen to make sure that people perform well at their jobs. Useful performance management communication is built around enabling employees to

- Understand job expectations
- Set goals
- Adjust and fine-tune their performance
- Stay accountable to expectations and goals
- Produce desired outcomes

Regular performance-oriented attention by the manager helps keep employees on track to fulfill expectations and produce desired outcomes. Regular conversations and periodic meetings for check-ins and feedback, measurement of employee outcomes, and documentation of progress and setbacks ensure a manager knows what's going on, can anticipate the next steps or needs of her team, and is rarely surprised by new developments or situations.[1]

THE WALTZ OF WORK: KEY STAGES OF PERFORMANCE MANAGEMENT

With manager–employee communication being the consistent medium, think of the performance management process as happening in three phases, reflected in the following figure.

Figure 8.1: Stages of Performance Management

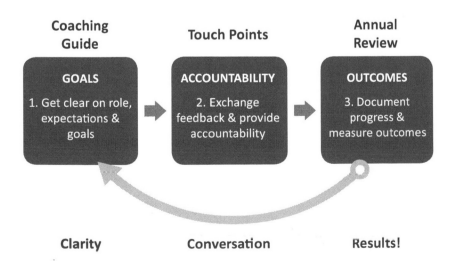

Now you may look at this model and say, "That's traditional." Yes, it is traditional, but with the capacity for managers to personalize it to their approach. How can you take the traditional model and add more touch points and really get to know the employee even better? How can these interactions allow growth and more success? The frequency with and manner in which these phases take place may vary from manager to manager. Some managers may have a style of managing spontaneously during office walk-throughs and lunch conversations, while others may choose a more formal approach of regular meetings. Some managers may engage in daily performance management conversations, while others choose a weekly, monthly, or quarterly approach. This is getting your mind on your people.

We can look to generational differences as the reason the need for constant feedback seems to be increasing. Keeping our young millennial talent engaged consistently so they don't leave is a concern. While such attention is critically important, we don't want to lose sight of the deeper conversations. It's not so much the structure in which these phases of performance management are executed that's important as it is that each of these areas be included along the way. They are learning and growing and it's not only time to give them feedback but to help them understand the why behind what's working and what's not.

Phase 1: The Coaching Guide: Getting Clear on Roles, Expectations, and Goals, Oh My!

It's launch time. Performance management begins as soon as the employee is hired. Remember those role profiles the team worked on together so painstakingly to make sure the organization hired the right people? That was the foundation for effective performance management. In this early phase of performance management, the manager should plan to set up an initial performance interview with the new employee—or the existing employee in a new role—and go over the role profile together. (This should be a natural part of the onboarding process discussed in chapter 6, but I mention it here too as it lays the foundation for effective performance management.)

more to get your mind on...

SIX STEPS TO BRINGING OUT THE TALENT YOU NEED FROM THE EMPLOYEES YOU HIRE

For a more in-depth model on how to hire and manage performance to bring out talent, visit www.loristohs.com /getyourmindon.

What are the expectations of the work, especially when employees are just starting? There is so much to learn. What are the desired outcomes? What goals do you want to create together to capitalize on employee strengths and to deliver outcomes? What are all the skills, experience, knowledge, and talents you know this employee has that will help him or her kick butt and do a great job? What's the employee's vision for this role? Does he have a special talent or insight that might justify a modification to the job to boost his performance beyond what was originally envisioned for the role? What talent does the person bring and how can she use that talent in the role? If you are aware of her talents and her style, understanding this can help you set her up for success and get her ramped up even more effectively. How do you and the employee envision the employee spending her time in the role? Do you share this time allocation vision? What a great way to engage your employee!

Remember the assessments you did on the front end. This is the perfect time to review them with the employee so your new hire can really feel valued. When placed within a context of the employee's strengths and resources, the performance launch can be an exciting time. When expectations are clear, employees have a place to direct the motivation and energy they often feel at the start of a new job.

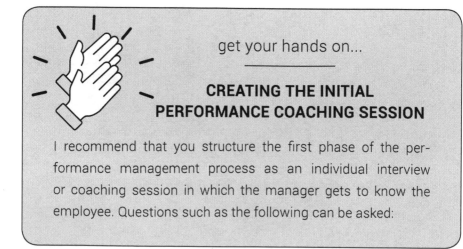

get your hands on...

CREATING THE INITIAL PERFORMANCE COACHING SESSION

I recommend that you structure the first phase of the performance management process as an individual interview or coaching session in which the manager gets to know the employee. Questions such as the following can be asked:

- "What do you do best?"
- "What are some areas that you will need help managing?"
- "In what areas would you like to grow and develop?"
- "What motivates you?"
- "What do you expect of me as your manager?"
- "How often do you think we should meet?"

No matter what kind of performance management system is used at the organization, every manager should start with a get-to-know-you conference of this sort.

During this interview, it's important for the manager to work with the employee to set goals too. This would come after reviewing the role profile with the employee and getting clear on expectations.

Note that it's not just the manager's goals that matter here. The tasks and duties for the role are the reason the role exists, so of course those need to be set and discussed. Yet, to get an employee to feel invested and like a valuable member of the team (and also to help you gain some insights into the employee), it's wise to have that employee inject his thoughts, insights, and ambitions into the process by suggesting his own goals.

I will ask, "What goals would you like to accomplish in the next however many days?" In the next stage (phase 2) of the performance management process, the manager and employee will review how the progress toward meeting these goals is coming along so that the manager can hold the employee accountable as well as provide support and feedback.

Phase 2: Staying Checked In: Time for Feedback and Accountability

Once expectations are clear and goals have been set, the manager can help the employee stay on track through periodic, regular check-ins. Whether these occur during office walk-arounds, lunch get-togethers, or scheduled meetings, the check-in phase of performance management involves information gathering, providing feedback, and accountability reality checks. The manager is continually ready to ask questions and listen for the answers. What is going well for the employee? Not so well? How is she coming along on goals? Kudos can be given for on-time deliverables. Are they spending the time expected on the project areas? Is it taking longer than expected? What happened in cases where timelines and goals weren't met?

Think of the information-gathering part of performance management as the "how's it going?" phase of the process. It's a chance to have real conversations with the employee on a regular basis that allow for a natural flow of information that the manager can use to facilitate performance toward positive outcomes. This may include asking what's going on for the employee at home as much as it is about asking what's going on at work. "How's the new baby?" "How are you liking this city?" "How is your nonprofit work going?" Not only does this kind of caring build important relationship trust that can be drawn on in the future, work life and personal life are often inextricably connected. A sick and aging parent at home may explain lateness to Monday morning meetings.

Being aware of an employee's upcoming move into a new home may provide valuable insight into when not to schedule the annual retreat. Remember we care about the employee as a whole person. Whole person engagement leads to higher performance.

Next, let's look at the feedback piece. It can include everything from motivational feedback ("Great job!") to improvement feedback ("I really like how you were creative on that design. Are you able to size it to fit the different mediums?") Think of feedback as a continual loop, meaning managers are regularly having conversations with individuals about the work they are doing and how the individuals are faring.

> **Whole person engagement leads to higher performance.**

To be effective, it is important that feedback be consistent too. When we give consistent feedback, we build trust. When trust is built, there is more opportunity for dialogue on new ideas, more support when there is failure, and ideally fewer mishaps because there is constant communication that leads to everyone being on the same page. Just as it's common for you to think you have been clear, how another person interpreted what you said may not be the same as what you were thinking.

For example, I had a leader, Carrie, who was always disappointed in her team's work. Her continual displeasure with their output dragged them down. They never felt good enough, ever. They felt like they never got their work right. While observing their group's interactions, I realized that Carrie thought she was

> **When we give consistent feedback, we build trust. When trust is built, there is more opportunity for dialogue on new ideas, more support when there is failure, and ideally fewer mishaps because there is constant communication that leads to everyone being on the same page.**

being clear with the team when she communicated with them, but she really wasn't. In looking at her style, I found that she was very visual and conceptual, but those images she had in mind didn't always come across in her words. I suggested that the solution to the disconnect between what she visualized and what she communicated to the team was for her to draw pictures of what she was thinking. This way, if her words were not clear, the team could possibly (and literally!) see what she was asking them to produce via her illustrations. I also had her ask her team at the end of each meeting to repeat back what they were going to do. This way, we knew the gaps in understanding were minimized.

When giving employees feedback, it's important for the feedback loop to go both ways, too. As much as managers need to be providing feedback to employees, managers also need to regularly ask employees how they are performing. They can lead the conversation with a start, stop, and continue method. What does the employee feel would be helpful for the manager to start doing, stop doing, and continue doing? This approach creates a feedback loop of trust through dialogue and relationship building. Oh, and just a little hint, this start, stop, and continue method works in many types of relationships.

Think of this part of the job as coaching, with a little counseling thrown in for good measure. Young employees might not always know what expected workplace behavior is, and older employees might assume, having proven themselves to be valuable, contributing members of the organization, that they are beyond having to play well with others. If someone is producing at work like gangbusters but has a horrible attitude that brings down the office, thereby depressing the output of the rest of the team, that needs to be called out in feedback sessions, too. While it's not fun for the manager to have to highlight a poor attitude, the possible pain of doing so in the short-term is worth the long-term gains of nipping bad behavior in the bud and creating a more positive work environment for the whole team.

Finally, there's accountability—checking in with the employee to see if work that the individual committed to did indeed get done. When an employee has met objectives, the manager's accountability check-in provides a chance to provide positive feedback and reinforce the performance, increasing the chances for repeat positive performance in the future. When employees have not met objectives, the accountability check-in provides a chance to get clear on what obstacles and challenges may have gotten in the way of the desired performance so they can be addressed.

The benefits of accountability aren't limited to enhanced individual performance. As noted by performance coach Craig

Lewis, "Research consistently contends that business leaders lose most kudos when poor performance is left unattended and poor performers are able to continue their inappropriate behaviour without repercussion."[2] In organizations where employees are held accountable, everyone knows that they can count on their coworkers to deliver on their commitments and to pitch in when problems arise, which creates a culture of trust and support rather than one in which everyone is simply looking to cover their own backside. People aren't wasting time stewing about how Evan never delivers on any of his assignments, manager Raina never calls him to the carpet on it, and the rest of the department always has to pick up the slack.

> **What does the employee feel would be helpful for the manager to start doing, stop doing, and continue doing? This approach creates a feedback loop of trust through dialogue and relationship building.**

Rather, as noted by accountability expert Mark Samuel, "When people are accountable to each other, the resulting synergy creates new solutions that no one person could have developed. . . . They implement goal solutions effectively. . . . They accomplish their results in half the time expected, because of the participation and commitment of everyone as a team. . . . People feel supported during the most difficult times, whether it is dealing with a work-related situation or a personal challenge that, even peripherally, affects their work. If you want to find an example of an accountable organization, look for any winning basketball team, dance company, symphony orchestra or any organization that is exceeding expectations against all odds."[3]

Within this context, you can see how accountability is not wielded as a form of punishment, it's about creating a structure that sets individuals up for success and an organizational culture that recognizes the importance of individuals delivering on their promises. Whether you are an individual performer, a manager, or an executive, it's human nature to be more likely to do things you say you will do when you know someone will be checking in and following up. The entire life coaching and executive coaching industry has been built on this premise. Accountability leads to results. By weaving accountability into ongoing project management, managers can make it a natural part of the process that allows for tweaks and adjustments to performance—and even the deadline itself, if necessary—along the way.

A manager who holds the employee accountable builds credibility and respect with employees. If nothing happens when a deadline goes flying by and the work isn't done, what's going to happen when the next deadline arises? We can't be sure, but it will likely not be a flurry of work. If you want your employees to do what they say they will, when they say they will, holding them accountable with well-timed check-ins offers a great support to them.

How often should these check-ins occur after the initial performance conference (phase 1)? I call them touch points and like to do them every 90 days (beyond doing the weekly check-in work conversations), providing enough time for the employee to attain his stride but not so long that unmet objectives go unnoticed. At the 360-day mark, it's time for the full performance review that aligns with organizational strategies, goals and outcomes.

The employee isn't the only one who needs to be held accountable. Managers at all levels need to get together on a regular basis to discuss how they are aligning their teams to keep them accountable for the overall business strategy. Remember the Human Capital Optimization model. Your teams are ostensibly implementing the strategies you agreed to use to accomplish your goals as an organization, but how often are you sitting down to consciously assess whether you are still aligned with your intended goals? Doing this takes time, but it is essential.

When I am brought in to help companies with strategic planning in their organizations, we find that many times before setting strategy, we have to first step back, evaluate existing pieces, and clean house. Organizations often get blown off course because they have inadvertently been responding to the noise and flurry of everyday life and have not consciously stopped to reevaluate whether circumstances have redirected the organizational ship toward an uncharted island rather than the paradise they'd originally targeted.

Phase 3: How'd We Do? Measuring Progress and Outcomes

Now we come to the phase of performance management that most people are familiar with: the annual performance review. Year-end check in. Performance review. Annual review. Whatever you choose to call the manager's meeting with direct reports to

more to get your mind on...

SETTING UP GUARDRAILS TO WORK WITH AN EMPLOYEE'S PERFORMANCE WEAKNESSES

If Chatty Kathy is in sales and produces great numbers while doing a poor job on documenting her travel expenses, that can be a painful problem for the Accounting Department. But if she's meeting or exceeding her sales quota, it doesn't make sense to let her go. Detailed Darren may need to do research in his role, but it becomes clear during his feedback touch points that he goes too far down the rabbit hole and doesn't get the final work done. Hmmm. Guess he has those great strengths of learner and input. By learning how to build the right guardrails for an employee, managers can help individuals navigate areas of nonstrengths. To learn more about how to set up these guard-rails, go to www.loristohs.com/getyourmindon.

discuss past progress and performance, the question is, "Do your employees fear the annual performance review, or do they look forward to it? I understand that some employees may be apprehensive about their performance review and the documentation that comes with it, but if done right, the whole process of providing feedback can actually be an empowering experience for employees. In fact, this can be a natural culmination of the entire performance management process if you've done goal setting and feedback well.

Instead of dreading the time it takes to put the annual performance report together, the manager can build on paperwork and meetings generated throughout the year to create the annual performance review. The employee, normal nerves aside, can anticipate the nature of the meeting based on the ongoing performance management conversations throughout the year. Surprises are far less common in the annual performance review when they build on a year's worth of regular goal setting, accountability, and feedback.

Phase 3 of the performance management process is about measuring an individual on her performance in the role. It's when we give him or her a scorecard (figurative, although it could be literal) to answer the question of "How are you doing?" The ultimate goal for each employee is to achieve success, of course, but what exactly is success, and how is it reflected on the scorecard? I see success as consisting of three things: your employee is

- engaged,
- achieving business outcomes or otherwise contributing to the bottom line, and
- filling the role profile productively.

Ideally, the employee shows up with success in all three areas; if not, it's clear where adjustments need to be made in the year to come.

Performance reviews can become more complicated if your organization is structured as a work matrix—if individual employees work with two or three different managers or on different teams, it's important to include feedback from others who are involved in working closely with that individual at each stage, and especially the final one.

Here's an example. At a health care startup I worked with, the nurses were a part of a nursing team, so they could share best practices and grow in their role by learning from each other, but they primarily worked with their physician. Making the physician a part of the performance review process was essential. Including those key constituents is important, because they are best positioned to know or even set the expectations of what is to be done, and they are then able to evaluate the application and performance of those expectations.

One best practice in a different client organization was that we created an internal customer survey of all constituents who worked with each individual. Those constituents included the direct manager, any key customers, and peers. Because feedback was coming from many people who worked with an individual, this helped the person being reviewed to no longer feel like his professional fate rested on a single person's subjective judgment.

We carefully designed questions that aligned to our values, our culture, and the work being done. We also included a few open-ended questions that allowed the employee to receive substantive, explanatory feedback. This also allowed the employee to see truly honest and direct comments about themselves—confidentially, of course. It also helped the managers to validate their observations as well as to see what patterns were consistent. Oh, and remember the selection and development assessments on the front end we discussed? If we were to take a peek at this feedback and their assessments, there would be a high correlation between the two.

When I think of the annual performance review, I don't see it as a scary thing to be feared. I see it as the opposite: something to get excited about, something to embrace! The annual performance report strikes me as being a tangible demonstration of everything the employee has created and accomplished during the year. Year after year, this folder of accomplishment expands.

Imagine being able to pull from the drawer or your electronic records a file folder of well-done performance reviews that looked back over your entire career and showed where you started, what goals you set, how you accomplished them, where you challenged yourself to do more, how you grew, and what your legacy was. Wow! That could be so valuable, not to mention rewarding. It also helps the employee to understand who they truly are and where their world-class performance comes from. Look at all of those patterns of success and where partnerships need to exist.

It requires a shift in thinking to see the review this way: from the fear of failure to the freedom to try, explore, grow, and create. It's a shift from a worry like, "What if there are black marks on my record or I'm seen as doing something wrong?" to "What will I get to try next now that I've proven myself by achieving what I was challenged to do?" The annual performance review, when done well and as part of the continual performance management process, isn't punitive. It's about accomplishment and development. How

more to get your mind on...

_____

YOUR HANDY PERFORMANCE MANAGEMENT CHECKLIST

A culture of feedback is an essential part of effective performance management. As employees move through their work, good managers provide feedback and hold employees accountable for meeting expectations: What was done and how was it done? Cheerfully? Begrudgingly? Are accolades in order or is an attitude adjustment needed? What wasn't done and why? What are the consequences for something not being completed, and how can things be adjusted to help ensure desired outcomes in the future? As you can imagine, there are many ways to effectively manage performance. Depending on the manager, the employee, the workplace, the team, and the job role, to name a few variables, the specifics of the process can look quite different. Yet, the core tenets are fairly standard, or at least a good springboard from which to launch yourself into your own, specific milieu. To learn these core tenets and see a performance-management checklist, go to www.loristohs.com/getyourmindon.

exciting it can be to see what you have done for the organization over the course of your time there.

HELPING EMPLOYEES FLEX THEIR MUSCLES

To get the most out of the performance management process, let's remember what's at the very center of the Human Capital Optimization Model: strengths-based development. As managers move through each phase of performance management—from goal setting to feedback to assessing outcomes—an evaluation of each individual performer's strengths will provide great insight into the reason behind performance wins versus letdowns. It will help demystify the reasons why goals were met success-fully so the strategies can be replicated in the future and provide data points for disappointments so adjustments can be made to increase performance.

Also, keep in mind that managers and other organizational leaders are individual performers too, which means that they, like everyone else, need reviews to make sure they are staying on track and are en route to meeting their goals. Manager reviews espe-cially are an easy thing to miss in the middle of all the feedback they're dishing out, but what's sauce for the goose is sauce for the gander. Plus, remember that feedback is a good, positive thing. Feedback is not a punishment but an opportunity; it's not fair to withhold that kind of learning tool from an employee just because that employee holds a spot on the corporate ladder more closely associated with giving reviews than getting them.

In fact, because managers affect the work lives of so many people, an argument can be made that it's even more important for them to receive feedback so as to keep them aligned with the organizational culture and goals. Given that employees leave man-agers, not jobs, it behooves the organization to review manager performance regularly to ensure that individual managers aren't a consistent factor in employee attrition.

Figure 8.2: Human Capital Optimization Model Close-Up:
Management and Performance Management of Existing Employees

- Role Clarity
- Expectations
- Accountability
- Training
- Development
- Performance Management

get your hands on...

APPLYING STRENGTHS-BASED PERFORMANCE MANAGEMENT

A use of strengths-based development throughout the performance management process might look something like this:

- *Discovery interview*. Review what the individual's strengths are and see how they align with the role profile and job expectations; set goals accordingly and realistically; think about where support may need to be called in to supplement less strong areas or what structures and guidelines may need to be put in place.

- *Weekly touch points*. Check in with your employees weekly to be sure you are aligned on progress on projects, giving any needed direction, providing feedback, and communicating expectations or new information needed to keep on track with each other. Don't forget to ask what you can do to support them. Oh, and say "thank you!"

- *Quarterly conversations*. As you check in and learn about the individual's wins and challenges, be mindful of her strengths and how they have an impact on performance; for goals not met, consider how a lack of strength in this area may have contributed and what guardrails may need to be put into place to help the individual in the future; for expectations met or exceeded, is this a sign that the individual should be given more work along these lines to play to strengths and create even greater output?

- *Annual review*. When interpreting the individual's yearly performance scorecard, expect to see patterns of results based on strengths. Consistency in strength areas equals world-class performance. Celebrate strengths and don't assume that weak spots are insurmountable obstacles. If performance lags in certain areas, it's time to assess whether the individual needs new guardrails, additional support and resources, a revised role profile, or a transfer into a new area of the organization.

When you take a strengths-based approach to managing individuals, you dispel with illusions around what you might wish the person would be in the role (but never will be) and deal with how the person truly is and always will be at work. We know from the Whole Person Model (see chapter 3 as well as the following "What to Do with a 'Problem' Employee" text box in this chapter) that experience, skills, and knowledge can be gained, but not so with strengths. By managing with this reality in mind—that individuals either have strengths or they don't have them—managers can guide and coach individuals in ways that leverage the individuals' strengths and work around their weaknesses. Like the maestro of the orchestra bringing the distinct sounds of various instruments together to make the desired music, the manager can also leverage strengths of different team members to achieve desired outcomes.

When I think about the strengths-based performance process, I am reminded of the notes we all got on our grade school report cards. You know the ones: the extra comments from your teacher about your behavior that had the power to neutralize your parents' praise for your good grades. "Yeah, I see you got all *A*'s and *B*'s, but what is this about you talking in class?" The chatty people, who talk a lot now and certainly did even more when younger and more impulsive, have grown up to become great at teaching, communicating, speaking, and sales, because communicating is their natural talent. That natural talent, for which they got grief in grade school, has gotten them far in this world!

In a similar way, the people who are the brightest idea people— who are conceptual and who get things—they were the ones who got the report card notes that they were daydreaming, looking out the window, and were not involved in class. Yet, that deep thinking, once harnessed in the work world, has led to incredible inventions, breakthroughs, and art.

So the job falls to managers to identify, develop, and harness an individual's talents. Ostensibly, this is for the good of the organization that the manager and employee both work for. But take a moment to remember how great you feel when you do something that really taps into what interests you and just comes naturally. As I mentioned in chapter 1, psychologist Mihaly Czikszentmihalyi calls activity that is so all-engrossing that a person loses track of time *flow* and identifies it as the key to happiness.[4]

Imagine designing an employee's role profile in a way that fits your employee's talents so well that work becomes the key to that person's happiness. What a privilege that would be! This is why great managers are worth their weight in gold and truly the unsung heroes not just of the workplace but of society. This flow—this engagement at work for all employees—is what the Human Capital Optimization Model is intended to achieve.

WHAT TO DO WITH A "PROBLEM" EMPLOYEE: WHOLE PERSON MODEL TO THE RESCUE

It's a frustrating scenario that every manager has faced: an employee who is simply not performing. What's going on? More important, how do you fix this problem? Take a deep breath and a step back, then look to the Whole Person Model (see Figure 3.1

in chapter 3) for help. You'll need to consider your employee as a whole to figure out how to make this situation better. Don't be afraid to jump in, ask questions, and get involved in this situation: confronting a problem is a constructive thing, and it doesn't have to involve being confrontational. Keep an eye on your end goal of engagement for your employee. Remember, it's very likely you're not the only one unhappy in this situation. If an employee is underperforming, that employee is, at best, disengaged and possibly actively disengaged. It's time to take constructive action to make work better for both of you, as well as the department and the organization!

Begin by determining whether the issue is the employee's skills, knowledge, experience, talent, or values. Does your employee need to be taught more skills? Does your employee need to attain more knowledge? Maybe your employee has never before done what you're giving him to do, so he doesn't have experience. Maybe the work you are expecting from your employee does not tap into any of the employee's innate talents, so the employee's output is slow or lackluster. Or perhaps your employee's values get in the way of your expectations: If your office's claim to fame is fast turnaround but the employee comes from a tradition of "anything worth doing is worth doing perfectly, even if it's late," that collision of values is going to cause a problem.

Once you've identified the source of the problem, figure out what you can do about it. Does your employee not know what he or she should be doing? Would a class or sessions with a trainer address the issue at hand? Has this employee shadowed someone else who was completing a similar task? If you have trained and retrained and provided the person with opportunities to perform the task and he is still not able to perform, it's probably a talent issue. Remember, you can't teach talent!

If the issue is a lack of natural talent for the problematic work responsibility, some mental calculations are in order. We clearly have a gap. So the first question to ask is the following.

1. What percentage of the person's job does this problematic component represent? Are we talking 10 percent, 20 percent, or 50 percent? Obviously depending on the percentage, this will determine the action. If it's 50 percent or more, this is likely not the right role for the person.

2. If it's something you can manage, how do you manage the gap?
   - Look at her strengths and think about how this individual can approach this part of her work using a natural strength.
   - Encourage the employee to set up a system for dealing with this troublesome task.
   - Do a task swap. Find a partner who can work with this individual and possibly swap some of the individual's role with someone who has the talent and this individual may be able to take some of the other person's work in the areas that she herself performs well.

Finally, it's up to you as the manager to set up some guidelines to help the employee streamline the part of the job that's tripping him or her up. Set up the parameters of the task early, and don't forget to define the percentage of time the employee should allot for that part of the role. If you notice an employee is taking an inordinate amount of time to do some research, the manager may need to provide a guideline on how many hours should be devoted to this kinds of task in the future. If this doesn't address the issue, perhaps this task is simply not right for the employee given her talents. (Remember that jobs that don't come naturally often consume a disproportionate number of work hours that could be devoted to more engaging work.)

If a large percentage of the role is not speaking to your employee's talents, then your employee may need to be repositioned to a role more in line with what comes naturally to him or her. Be sure, though, to handle the transition with sensitivity and dignity. This should not be seen as a defeat or failure but a repositioning to amplify the employee's abilities for the good of the employee and the organization.

Remember: when you're having a problem with an employee, refer back to the Whole Person Model (for a refresher, see chapter 3): it can help illuminate where to start looking in the areas of development. Addressing the problem with a good idea of what comprises its solution will make for a better work experience for both you and your (formerly problematic) employee.

CONCLUSION: FINE-TUNING FOR WORLD-CLASS PERFORMANCE

When you get your mind on your human capital, it becomes even clearer how the time invested in keeping your people on track through effective performance management can pay dividends. Employees know what is expected of them and how they need to perform to effectively fill the role. They can take the regular feedback they receive to fine-tune their performance and generate more of what's working well. They feel seen and affirmed; they are able to do their best work; and this all translates into energy, engagement, and world-class results that distinguish you from your competitors and keep your clients—and your employees—coming back to an organization that they love.

THE EVOLUTION OF
THE REVOLUTION

World-Class Outcomes for Today and the Future

Where are you on the spectrum of human capital consciousness? How much do you value your people, and do they know it and feel it? Does this consciousness show up in the way you structure new job roles, who you promote, and how you manage talent at your organization? What matters most is that you have awakened to a higher awareness of the role you play. The movement has begun.

It's time to ask too: What is really on the inside? How would your customers describe the soul of your organization? Do they know that you have an honorable mission and vision and that you and your team are working hard every day to fulfill it? When your intentions are good, employees and customers feel it. They trust you, even when there are occasional mistakes in performance because they know that your business has a healthy pulse—a soul. You must have a purpose beyond a profit

As I drive by the office buildings in cities during my work and personal travel, I will now do more than wonder what is going on behind those four walls, asking whether people are being appreciated for who they are. Is the dialogue different? Are they comfortable waking up to real conversations that should be had? I will be smiling with a sense of hope that we all have a chance to do work that we love *and* that it serves the organization and its customers.

This can be achieved using the models provided in this book, models that integrate the needs of the organization with the needs of individual employees so that each serves the other in a potent brew that feeds clients, communities, and the world at large. Engaged employees lead to engaged and loyal customers. These customers contribute to successful financials. Employees contributing to the success of their organization by using their talent leads to fulfilled employees returning to their friends and family and making a positive impact in their homes and communities. Positive workplaces encourage healthy psychological capital, things like confidence, hope, optimism, and resiliency.[1]

The Human Capital Movement contributes not just to bettering organizations but to bettering our world.

With these tools at your disposal—the Human Capital Optimization Model, the Whole Person Model, Get Your Hands On exercises, More to Get Your Mind on web bonus material, and more—your organization now has a launching pad to optimize your human capital and achieve your organization's mission. I encourage you to use this book as a reference in the future in any way that it serves you, including to help you:

- Understand the impact of engagement versus disengagement at work (chapter 1)
- Align your business foundation (organizational culture, leadership, strategy, and brand) with your people strategy to fulfill the organization's mission (chapter 2)
- Employ and retain world-class employees that fit the job, the team, the manager, and the organization, using the Whole Person Model (chapter 3)
- Create job profiles to attract candidates with the right talent for a job (chapter 4)
- Increase the pool of qualified candidates you can draw from to fill empty positions (chapter 5)
- Customize onboarding to meet the needs of your people and to build company brand and culture from the start (chapter 6)
- Revolutionize the effectiveness of management by hiring only those individuals with the talent to manage and not

allowing them to get eaten up by distracting project work (chapter 7)

- Get the best out of your people by using the right performance management techniques (chapter 8)

- Get the most out of your people to achieve desired organizational outcomes and give back to your people so they can be happy human citizens who contribute to their families, communities, and the world

Whether you consume the whole enchilada or take baby bites of the Human Capital Optimization Model, this experience will take time. This is not the conclusion of the process; it is the beginning. Give your organization time to experience the evolution of the human capital revolution. I am reminded of a design firm I have been working with. Bit by bit, they have been putting the building blocks of the Human Capital Optimization Model in place, and it has been exciting to see the real-world benefits.

> **This is not the conclusion of the process; it is the beginning.**

Their story involves one company in multiple geographies. The Western division had been working with us for several years, while the Eastern Division didn't feel they needed human capital support. Their revenue was higher, after all. Great for them! Yet, what worried me was that the Eastern Division had high turnover and lower engagement than the Western Division. What I knew and tried to help the Eastern Division understand was that people metrics are *leading indicators*, whereas financial metrics like revenue are *lagging indicators*. If the people metrics aren't good, eventually the financial metrics will catch up to reflect problems—after it's too late to solve the issues without financial fallout. In short, you need to get to the root cause of the issues your employees are having before these issues become reflected in the bottom line.

It wasn't until the Eastern Division began to have a challenge with one particular leader that they decided to try using this approach. I have watched their organization start to shift. When they first started working with us, the unit's delivery performance had slipped and their people were not happy. We worked together to help the company focus on the business side of the Human Capital Optimization model (including leadership and strategy), as well as the people side. In doing so, we discovered that the Eastern Division needed to get their strategy and leadership aligned and the right people in the right roles in order to accomplish their strategy.

On the basis of some of the changes we made, low performers started to select themselves out and depart the organization. The CEO of the Eastern Division retired, and the group rearranged the chairs of the leadership team. As a result, we have started to see shifts in the culture. Although there was some immediate turnover, employee engagement numbers are increasing, turnover decreasing, and better dialogue and communication taking place. Before we used the model, necessary and important conversations simply weren't happening. Now they are happening in an effective way.

I will never tire of having those goose-bump moments when I see leaders and staff have that "aha" moment when they discover that it's really all about the people. One of these moments happened recently when I worked with a group of leaders to roll out a new strategic plan to their teams as they prepared for the retirement of their leader. While some organizations simply email their staff to inform them of new strategy, we dedicated an entire day to getting the team members informed and invested in the new strategy.

The full day of activities began with a discussion of employee strengths. As we had been building a strengths-based culture, we had listed each person's strengths on wall-sized paper and table tents at their table, based on their earlier assessment results. As employees entered the room and the meeting began, they could see in full display what each person was great at and how they all brought something unique to the team. Next, in order to help people connect their roles to the work—to the strategic plan—we invited them to head to the strategic plans on the wall and and mark the areas they were interested in with dots regarding where they wanted to be involved.

By the time the day was done, I knew we had successfully created connection and commitments based on the enthusiasm and energy in the room. My favorite moment was when we asked each person to share their biggest discovery from the day. Answers were consistent: employees described how they had discovered the power of culture and of having the right people in the organization. Whether it was a 28-year-old millennial, a three-time boomerang, or a Baby Boomer who responded, the sentiment was the same: culture is important and it is really all about the people!

The final touching moment for me of this experience came later that week when I observed the outgoing leader, John, have an exchange with Jennifer, an outgoing employee who was leaving the organization for a job with fewer hours so she could have more time to spend with her family.

"Congratulations!" John said to Jennifer. "We are so excited for you. Family first. And you know we are here for you if you ever need us." I smiled thinking about how generous of spirit John was being with Jennifer—how in tune he was to his human capital—and I knew this was why the organization had so many boomerangs who came back to work with them. It was a sharp contrast to another organization that I worked with just up the street handling their people very differently by giving several staff members a pink slip and a box to pack their things and telling them to immediately leave the building. It showed quite the different value on their people.

Employees will come and go, for a variety of reasons. Honoring their value at every stage of the process, from onboarding to managing performance to departing, pays back dividends on so many levels, reflecting on the company brand, organizational culture, recruiting, retention, business results, and on and on...

Why align to this philosophy? My answer is this: I am hopeful your purpose goes beyond a profit. We the leaders of organizations can have a direct impact on people's lives and our world today.

Take a moment and check in with yourself. Do you have a soulful conscience? A human capital consciousness? How are you affecting the people in your organization? Are they clamoring to work for you and your organization? If not maybe it's time to make a change. Efforts to address delivery times, product quality, customer service procedures, or lean processes are important but will not be sustainable if you do not have a consciousness around your people. Join in the Human Capital Movement today.

One of my favorite benefits of the Human Capital Optimization Model is the way in which it helps organizations retain their superstar employees because they are well utilized and surrounded by other great performers. In this thriving environment, you can attract world-class performers because you are a great place to work—a place where people get to enjoy using their talents and see the positive outcomes of their efforts. You are able to keep your world-class people, too, because they like to work around other world-class performers. What's more, the old days of forcing your superstar performers into management roles they are not fit to take on just so they can keep rising in the company are gone with this model. Instead, the model encourages you to reward these employees with higher pay and expert or specialty roles that honor their talent, keeping them at the organization and leaving management roles to those who really have the talent to get the most out of people.

Figure 9.1: Human Capital Optimization Model Close-Up:
Outcomes of Strengths-Based Development

You may start using the Human Capital Optimization Model on a quest for improved financials and a better bottom line. When employees are engaged, they're more productive, you need fewer people because they do more work, your employees don't leave, turnover goes down, customers buy more because they're engaged more, the customers don't leave, your processes are cleaner and clearer, and you can see strategies fulfilled.

Also think about ways beyond your financials to define your

success. In the end, it may be the sustained intangibles of the Human Capital Movement that encourage you to use it over time:

- the gleam in an employee's eye as he uses his analytical skills to troubleshoot an IT issue,
- the laughter and vigorous chatter of a work group as they brainstorm how to launch your latest product, or
- the self-confidence an employee has gained because she finally has the right role for her,
- a room full of energized employees and their families at an appreciation event that celebrates their successes.

Join the movement. Increase your consciousness. Become an organization that everyone wants to work for—an organization with soul...a healthy soul.

Employees doing work that aligns with *their* talent and *your* strategy makes for a thriving work place and a thriving world.

Isn't it time we got started?

FIGURES AND TABLES

GET YOUR HANDS ON EXERCISES

MORE TO GET YOUR MIND ON WEB TOOLS

NOTES

CHAPTER 1

1. Epic. n.d. "Benefits: Sabbaticals." https://careers.epic.com/Home /Sabbatablog.
2. Adkins, Amy. 2016. "Employee Engagement in U.S. Stagnant in 2015." Gallup, January 13. http://news.gallup.com/poll/188144/employee engagement-stagnant-2015.aspx.
3. Ibid., 143.
4. Czikszentmihalyi, Mihaly. 2004. "Flow, the Secret to Happiness." Video, 18:55. TED2004. https://www.ted.com/talks /mihaly_csikszentmihalyi_on_flow.
5. Nink, Marco, and Jennifer Robison. 2016. "The Damage Inflicted by Poor Managers." *Gallup Business Journal*, December 20. http://www .gallup.com/businessjournal/200108/damage-inflicted-poor-managers. aspx.
6. Butterworth, Eric. 2001. *Spiritual Economics: The Principles and Process of True Prosperity.* Unity Village, MO: Unity Books, 100.
7. Ibid., 101.
8. Ibid., 105.
9. Luthans, Fred, Carolyn M. Youssef-Morgan, and Bruce J. Avolio. 2015. *Psychological Capital and Beyond.* New York, NY: Oxford University Press, 201.
10. Kruse, Kevin. 2013. *Employee Engagement for Everyone.* Philadelphia, PA: The Center for Wholehearted Leadership, 13.
11. Ibid., 14.

CHAPTER 2

1. Gallup. 2017. *State of the American Workplace.* http://www.gallup.com /reports/199961/state-american-workplace-report-2017.aspx, 61.
2. Ibid., 96.
3. Gentry, William A., Todd J. Weber, and Golnaz Sadri. 2007. *Empathy in the Workplace: A Tool for Effective Leadership.* White paper from the

Center for Creative Leadership. http://www.ccl.org/wp-content
/uploads/2015/04/EmpathyInTheWorkplace.pdf, 1.

4. "Culture." n.d. *Cambridge English Dictionary*. http://dictionary
.cambridge.org/dictionary/english/culture.

5. TOMS Shoes. 2016. "Improving Lives." http://www.toms.com
/improving-lives.

6. "We Are Shopify." n.d. *The Muse.* https://www.themuse.com
/companies/shopify.

7. Dr. Bronner's. n.d. "About." https://www.drbronner.com/about/.

8. "Dick Raines, President of CARFAX: Lessons from a Leader Rated Tops
Among Midsize Organizations." 2017. *The Washington Post Magazine:
Top Workplaces,* June 18, 22.

CHAPTER 3

1. Harter, James K., Frank L. Schmidt, Sangeeta Agrawal, Stephanie
K. Plowman, and Anthony Blue. 2016. *The Relationship Between
Engagement at Work and Organizational Outcomes: 2016 Q^{12} Meta-
Analysis* (9th ed.). Washington, DC: Gallup. http://www.gallup.
com/services/191489/q12-meta-analysis-report-2016.aspx?utm_
source=gbj&utm_medium=copy&utm_campaign=20160707-gbj.

2. Mitsch, Darelyn "DJ." 2016. *Zombies to Zealots: Reawaken the Human
Spirit at Work*. Bloomington, IN: Balboa Press.

3. Mankins, Michael, Alan Bird, and James Root. 2013.
"Making Star Teams Out of Star Players." *Harvard Business
Review,* January–February. https://hbr.org/2013/01
/making-star-teams-out-of-star-players.

4. Ibid.

CHAPTER 4

1. Boushey, Heather, and Sarah Jane Glynn. 2012. *There Are
Significant Business Costs to Replacing Workers*. Center for American
Progress. https://www.americanprogress.org/wp-content
/uploads/2012/11/CostofTurnover.pdf.

CHAPTER 5

1. Hauenstein, Patrick. n.d. *Common Employee Selection Tools: Trends and Recommendations.* White paper from OMNIview. http://www.theomniview.com/wp-content/uploads/white-papers/common_employee_selection_tools.pdf.
2. Ibid.
3. Brooks, Katharine. 2010. "The Simulation Job Interview." *Psychology Today Blog.* https://www.psychologytoday.com/blog/career-transitions/201012/the-simulation-job-interview.
4. Leibbrandt, Maika. 2013. "Why Being One in a Million Really Isn't that Special." *CliftonStrengths Coaching Blog.* Gallup, August 28. http://coaching.gallup.com/2013/08/why-being-one-in-million-really-isnt.html.

CHAPTER 6

1. Collins, Caroline. 2015. "Disney College Program Traditions Class." *Elly and Caroline's Magical Disney Moments* (blog), May 29. https://collinsrace1.wordpress.com/tag/disney-traditions/.

CHAPTER 7

1. Nink, Marco, and Jennifer Robison. 2016. "The Damage Inflicted by Poor Managers." *Gallup Business Journal,* December 20. http://www.gallup.com/businessjournal/200108/damage-inflicted-poor-managers.aspx.
2. Beck, Randall, and Jim Harter. 2014. "Why Great Managers Are So Rare." *Gallup Business Journal,* March 25. http://www.gallup.com/businessjournal/167975/why-great-managers-rare.aspx.
3. Ibid.
4. Ibid.
5. Buckingham, Marcus. 2005. "What Great Managers Do." *Harvard Business Review,* March. https://hbr.org/2005/03/what-great-managers-do.
6. Ibid.
7. Ibid.

CHAPTER 8

1. Rick, Torben. 2014. "A Simple Approach to High Performance Organization." *Meliorate* (blog), December 17. https://www.torbenrick.eu/t/r/eju.

2. Lewis, Craig. n.d. "A Small Hole Can Sink a Big Ship—The Poor Performer and Other Like Obstacles." http://www.evancarmichael .com/library/craig-lewis/A-Small-Hole-Can-Sink-A-Big-Ship--The-Poor-Performer-and-Other-Like-Obstacles.html.

3. Samuel, Mark. 2001. *The Accountability Revolution: Achieve Breakthrough Results in Half the Time!* Tempe, AZ: Facts on Demand Press, 6.

4. Czikszentmihalyi, Mihàly. 2004. "Flow, the Secret to Happiness." Video, 18:55. TED2004. http://www.ted.com/talks /mihaly_csikszentmihalyi_on_flow.

CHAPTER 9

1. Luthans, Fred, Carolyn M. Youssef-Morgan, and Bruce J. Avolio. 2015. *Psychological Capital and Beyond.* New York, NY: Oxford University Press.

ACKNOWLEDGEMENTS

Getting my mind on people is something I live every day. No one person can accomplish a movement like this on their own. Partners and support networks are necessary as we create a consciousness together by each bringing value and a perspective.

A big thank you goes to two of my partners over the past several months who have been by my side holding me accountable, helping me sort loads of information, listening patiently, and giving of themselves to the very last moment of launch, Suzanne and Stefanie from StyleMatters.

Suzanne, your ability to listen and capture the true essence of my writing and words and how to restate is amazing. Your patience and ability to ask deeper questions to understand my conceptual thinking is a great talent. You pulled the ball of yarn out of my brain and helped to make this is a crisp, practical, organized read.

Stefanie, your naturally quiet nature is such a gift. Your mind can capture so much information and dig deeper to find the right content to relay understanding of the message. Your ability to capture the details, and research, edit, and reference is amazing. Thanks for putting up with my schedule, letting me process and change my mind...more than once. You are both great writers, editors, mothers, and beautiful human beings. The hours and hours of time we spent together will never be forgotten.

The words of a book are the story but the story may not be read without the cover that catches the eye and the design elements to keep you engaged. Thank you, Jerry, for your talented eye for design. I appreciate your patience to hear and your conceptual capacity to understand my crazy ideas and bring them to life. The look, cover, and design elements are awesome! Thank you to my friend and mentor Doug, who made the obvious so obvious when deciding on my book name.

Learning the aspects of the book writing and publishing business can be a bit overwhelming. Thank you to Shanda from Transcendent Publishing for your time in educating me early on when this was just a thought. Your knowledge base of publishing and marketing has been so helpful. Your natural style of being open and sharing is such a gift to me and others. Thank you for your soulful teaching.

A good book is as good as its marketing. Thank you to Jamee for your creative mind and your ability to message words so beautifully in a way that reads our audience and to Ethan, thank you for your design expertise that captures the essence of the look and your video and audio knowledge to share messages with many. With your great work, we can reach more organizations and more leaders.

Thank you to my great team who is by my side every day making it all happen. Our clients are so appreciative of the well-oiled machine. Thank you for taking time to understanding and keeping all the balls in the air. Rhonda, Cathy, Maya, and Betsy, we are an awesome team.

To my coach Bill, who encouraged me and helped me to focus and not give up, and to my coach Lori, who has been encouraging me to do this for years. Thank you to you both.

To my clients who share so openly their stories and vulnerabilities and who have the desire to get their mind on their people, you are awesome and you are changing lives in your workplaces every day.

To my friends, Miekka, Jean, Michael, Lindsey Rai, Cindy, Rick, and Dee, who have stuck through this with me, listening to the thoughts and ideas for this book and giving me endless encouragement over the past months, thank you. Thank you, John, for allowing me to use your beautiful home, the spiritual space where I could focus and where God gave me the right words.

I couldn't have done this without the support from my two kids, Ethan and Emily. For the times I kept my head buried in writing and timelines, thanks for understanding. I am inspired by you to continue to be authentic and follow my dreams. I know you will both do that too.

My gratitude to all of you and many, many others who are beside me every day, for making this movement happen. I believe if this book does what it is set out to do, we will have touched many lives in a better way.

ABOUT THE AUTHOR

LORI STOHS is a builder of people, companies, and nonprofits. Her driving desire and her mission are to help organizations maximize their effectiveness through their most valuable asset, their human capital. As such, she specializes in strategic planning, human capital alignment, perfor-

mance management, organizational performance, selection and hiring, and strength-based development. Organizations that have made a successful impact through the use of Lori's philosophy include American Girl, Best Buy, Chick-fil-A, Discover, Marriott, Proctor & Gamble, Gensler, Perkins+Will, RDG Planning and Design, Interface, First Financial Credit Union, Union Pacific, American National Bank, and United Healthcare Group. Lori's years of impactful consulting with companies from all over the globe have helped move leaders and their teams to higher levels of performance.

Lori's talent is seeing an organization in a multidimensional way and using this viewpoint, helping leaders discover, understand, and sort through the noise and connect the dots. In the process, she helps them develop their unique strengths and talents and advises them on how to maximize performance. Her years of working with individuals and corporate teams have honed her ability to connect to a group of individuals by their strengths, immediately recognizing areas of success, potential pitfalls, and opportunities for growth. She is a world-class facilitator and translator who is able to bring things to the table that are many times the root cause of the challenge.

In addition to leading Lori Stohs Consulting Group, Lori has served as Chief People Officer at Think Whole Person Healthcare, a startup organization of 350 employees, creating culture, strengths-based hiring practices, and HR strategy and implementation. Before starting Lori Stohs Consulting in 2009, Lori served as a Global Account Executive for Microsoft. In her role, she consulted with companies to create technology solutions to meet business needs and strategic plans. Prior to her role at Microsoft, Lori served as a Principal at Gallup Consulting, a global research-based consulting firm, and Executive Director of Gallup University.

Community philanthropy is a priority for Lori and has always been a part of her life. Lori is a founding board member for Executives Without Borders, a global nonprofit organization. She is passionate about giving executive volunteers an engaging experience in working with nonprofit organizations as well as helping nonprofits increase their impact across the world. She is also a founding board member and facilitator for Leadership for Life, a faith-based leadership program. She was a founding board member for Social Impact Omaha, a nonprofit focusing on collaborative social responsibility. Her passion for impacting children and young adults is shown through her commitment to the Ronald McDonald House Charity Board and Hope Center for Kids Board.

Lori received her bachelor's degree in Business Administration and Management from the University of Nebraska—Lincoln and has continued as a lifelong student to grow her knowledge through various psychology, business, and human capital courses. She resides in Omaha, Nebraska.